//
SIX Days on a
PAPER BOAT

By: Jalyll Suarez

Copyright © 2023 by Jalyll Suarez, Six Days on a Paper Boat. Published through Rising Above Publishing Services

www.risingabovepublishing.com

All Rights Reserved. This book is a memoir. It reflects the author's present recollections of experiences over time. The information shared in this book represents experiences lived through by the author. Some names and characteristics have been changed, but no events or characters have been fabricated. The advice and strategies discussed may not be suitable for every situation. This book is intended to be informational only and is not intended to replace legal advice.

Photo credits for the front and back cover: Alberto Suarez

Paperback ISBN: 9798392867677

DEDICATION

To every young immigrant child, from the past, present, and future, reading these words, know that you are seen, valued, and cherished. May these pages be a source of inspiration, empowerment, and affirmation. May they remind you that you are not alone and that your journey, with all its triumphs and challenges, is a testament to the indomitable human spirit you carry. No matter where life takes you, embrace your roots, for they are the foundation upon which you will build a future filled with endless possibilities.

To the incredible single mothers who navigate the complexities of life with unwavering strength, resilience, and love. Your journey is one of courage, sacrifice, and determination, and this dedication is a small tribute to honor your unwavering devotion to your children. Your sacrifices may often go unnoticed, but they are deeply appreciated. As a single mother, you are the provider, the protector, and the comforter all rolled into one. The true source of love.

Which brings me to you, my dear Mother. I dedicate this book to you. There are really no words to fully describe how much I love, appreciate, and admire you, but I hope this book gives you a small glimpse of it. I love you Mom, with all my heart.

"There is no greater agony than bearing an untold story inside you."

- Maya Angelou

MESSAGE FROM THE AUTHOR

Who am I? This question has taken me on a lifelong journey that is still unfolding. It has caused a whirlwind of chaos and confusion. It has led me into my inner caves of darkness, forcing me to find the light myself. I've tried to ignore it, pretending it wasn't there, lingering in the back of my mind. I've tried to hide it, playing a part every day that I thought fit what I should be. I've denied and lied about it, even to myself- many times. Yet, it never went away until I stopped and owned it. My voice, my story, is a part of that process.

At my core, I am my Mother's son. I am the man that has the honor of continuing her legacy to hope for more, to have faith for more, and to believe in myself the way she has done all her life. I was shown at a young age what it meant to take a leap of faith. Mom risked everything, including our lives, to give us a new beginning- a fresh start. She refused to succumb to the world in Cuba that she was born into and held the hunger and thirst for more. Even though her ability was limited at times to what she could do, she held onto her beliefs and refused to relinquish her sight of the truth. She believed that life was more than being told what you can buy and when, what you can say and to who, what you can do, and where. She believed that there was an entirely different way of living in a new world and that it was possible for us to attain it, even though she didn't know how. She believed in our worthiness of freedom and knew that it was only distance that stood between us and actually having it.

I stood by her side on this journey of a new beginning and learned that believing and hoping for more costs a price many aren't willing to pay. I knew what it required to carry such a heavy responsibility. This torch was passed down to me during the six days it took to get to the new world. She took the risk. She faced death with her child for six days on a raft to give us more. She did her part. I knew it was up to me to now carry us further and achieve more. It wasn't something I took lightly, not even at eight years old when I first came to America.

The innocence of my childhood was blotted out at times with responsibilities and worries that most children don't have. I know, though, that there are those that understand. There are others who have also watched their parents risk everything for freedom. Who have watched them work their days and nights away just to put food on the table and all for one reason only- so that their children could have more opportunities. I know there are people that understand the responsibilities that come from your parents taking such a risk to have freedom. It overshadows every decision you make, creating an inner expectation of perfection that is nearly impossible. It is this expectation that has caused many battles within myself, fighting for what I wanted and what I thought was perfect. The farther I ran from myself, the farther I ran from the opportunities available to me. It has caused me to self-sabotage and hate myself out of the fear that I wasn't enough to carry this powerful torch that was handed to me. I hope that if you too can resonate with this that you are able to carry on your parents' legacy for more while also staying true to you as well. Both go hand in hand. It was within my own individuality that I was able to truly embrace the freedom my Mother risked everything for. I hope that my story sparks the fire you have been searching for to believe in yourself.

CHAPTER 1

THE BRIDGE OF IDENTITY

"When forms that you had identified with (like labels and roles), that gave you your sense of self, collapse or are taken away, it can lead to a collapse of the ego. When there is nothing to identify with anymore, who are you?"

excerpt from **A New Earth by Eckhart Tolle**

THE BRIDGE OF IDENTITY

There is a Japanese proverb that symbolically explains identity. It states that many people live a life wearing three faces. One face we show the world. The second face is the one we show those that live with us, the people closest to us. The last one is the face that is closest to our most authentic self, yet we only show this one to ourselves. This was my life for the first twenty-four years. The only time the face most true to me was able to come out was when I was alone in my room, and the only emotion I could feel was overwhelming sadness.

However, in the beginning, it wasn't always like that. I was once a happy-go-lucky little boy, always daydreaming but also very attentive. I would pay close attention to everything around me and was able to see the beauty in almost anything, from the way a cloud resembled familiar objects or animals, to a flower blooming out of a cracked pavement. Although, naturally, like all children, I was very naive. I was born in Havana, Cuba- a Libra baby. Weighing over nine pounds and a head full of black hair, I was my Mother's pride and joy from the moment we laid eyes on each other. An unbreakable bond was formed from the very first embrace. A bond that not even the strongest of storms could break.

THE BRIDGE OF IDENTITY

I grew up in the coastal town of Playa de Jaimanitas, Cuba, in the outskirts of Havana. Originally a fishing village. The innate beauty of my town counter-balanced the ugliness from the adverse living circumstances around us. I was a child of poverty. It was all I ever knew, so in a way, I was accustomed to hardship. Growing up in poverty is a challenging experience no matter where you are in the world, and this holds true for many individuals who grew up in Cuba, like me. The Caribbean island nation has a complex history, marked by economic struggles and political changes that have deeply impacted the lives of its citizens. While some progress has been made in recent years, poverty remains a significant issue for many Cubans, especially those who grew up in disadvantaged circumstances.

In Cuba, the concept of poverty often extends beyond the lack of material possessions. It encompasses limited access to basic necessities such as clean water, medication, and electricity. Fundamental items such as food, clothing, and household goods are always in short supply. We had to rely on the ration food system established by the government, which provided limited quantities of essential products at subsidized prices. This meant that there were long lines and uncertainty surrounding the availability of even the most basic goods. It was not uncommon for families to stand in line for hours, sometimes without the guarantee of obtaining what they needed. Housing conditions were another struggle for us growing up in poverty. Many families lived in cramped and deteriorating apartments or houses, often with multiple generations sharing limited space. Rundown buildings, lack of proper sanitation, and intermittent access to utilities were common issues. Overcrowding and substandard living conditions made it difficult to find privacy and a sense of security.

Education has always been highly valued in Cuba, but poverty often posed a significant obstacle to receiving a standard education. While primary and secondary education are free and accessible to all, the lack of resources impacted the quality of education available. Schools frequently lacked basic supplies, textbooks, and proper facilities. It requires creativity and determination for students and their families to overcome these challenges and pursue their educational goals. Access to healthcare is another area affected by poverty. While Cuba has made significant advancements in healthcare, including the development of medical treatments, and exporting doctors to other countries, the system still faces limitations due to resource constraints. People also find difficulties in accessing medical services, obtaining necessary medications, and receiving timely and adequate care. Many hospitals are in deplorable conditions, experiencing critical shortage of medical equipment and supplies, even down to the basics such as having clean paper sheets to cover the metal beds. Many of them have broken windows and no air conditioning. Aside from having to deal with the issues that originally brough them to the hospitals, families are also having to bring mosquito netting to combat the outbreak of deadly mosquito transmitted diseases while staying in the hospital. Growing up poor in Cuba meant facing all these hardships on a daily basis, and it required resilience, resourcefulness, and a strong sense of community to navigate through life's challenges.

I lived a simple life, but what made it beautiful, and fulfilling was my family. I grew up with lots of cousins and many of us were around the same age, so we did things together all the time, even though I was one of the youngest in the group. Together we would play for hours on end. Our favorite pastime included reenacting folklore action films. We would become archers, ninjas and swordsmen and take our time creating bows and arrows, swords made of wood and ninja outfits. Whatever the latest film or show was at the time, we would try recreating it and get lost in our make-believe world.

I would find comfort in being in my Aunt Angela's house. Her home was a revolving door for everyone in the family. The matriarch of all my aunts, as the oldest, she had a way of keeping us all together. I would wake up every Saturday and head over to her house to watch the Saturday morning cartoons. Mom and I didn't own a television so I would spend hours at my auntie's house watching tv or playing outside her porch with my cousins. My aunt would put her record player on with the sounds of legendary singers, like Julio Iglesias, Juan Gabriel, Roberto Carlos, and so many others, blasting the whole neighborhood with their iconic voices—sweet memories that to this day brings a smile to my face. My aunt also loved baking and making sugary lollipop-like sweets such as "piruli" and "chambelonas" to sell in the neighborhood and she would always let me have some. My weekly nights consisted of falling asleep next to my Mother, usually on the floor of one of my aunt's houses, since it was the coolest spot and no one had air conditioning, as we watched Spanish-translated Brazilian telenovelas religiously. Strangely, for a long period of time, every single night while I fell asleep mid-way through the telenovela, I would have nightmares. The exact same nightmare. I would see myself tiny, astral projecting across a tremendous amount of endless open space, being tossed around in what I can only describe as water molecules, like being swept away by waves back and forth. Many times, I woke up in a panic, crying.

Life for a kid in Cuba during the 80's was, for the most part, carefree, where even the first sound of rain drops felt like a natural force inviting us to run outside to play under the rain. Weekly power outages were a norm, and we made the best of it as a people. If the outage happened to be at night, the neighborhood folks would congregate out on the block. While the adults gossiped, us kids would run around collecting fireflies. Even though on the surface I seemed content around people, something inside of me prevented me from fully being present and truly happy. I just didn't know what it was.

From the time I can remember, I didn't walk how the other boys walked. I didn't feel any attraction to girls, even though I knew I was supposed to. I didn't know what it meant as a child, but I knew I was different. Despite knowing this, I had never paid much attention to it. I quickly dismissed it as a passing thought without ever giving much energy to think as to why I felt that way. I was

THE BRIDGE OF IDENTITY

a young child and hadn't met that part of myself yet. That is until it was forced upon me to recognize something in me that I wasn't ready to meet.

During one of the visits with my dad, he pointed something out to me that he probably didn't think much of past that day, but his words have had a significant impact on me, even to this day. You see, my Mom and dad and I never lived together as a happy family. I only saw my dad when he visited his mother, my grandmother, in the same town I lived in or when I would go visit him where he lived, in another province within Cuba. In fact, I didn't really know my dad until I was three years old, but I'll get into that later. Even though I didn't get to spend a lot of time with my dad, I still looked up to him. Besides my grandfather, he was the only other man I had as a role model, and his strong presence played a significant role in my life- up until that one day.

I was always excited to see him every time he came into town. I made my way to my grandmother's house once I got news of his arrival because he had sent for me to see him. My excitement was almost uncontainable, and I eagerly rushed over to my grandmother's house, which was on a large estate along with several other homes. As

THE BRIDGE OF IDENTITY

I approached the entrance from the street, I could see her house at the back end of the property. I rounded the corner and then saw my dad sitting on the front porch of her home. I started walking towards him with a massive smile on my face. I couldn't wait to hug him, but before I could, my dad got up from his chair and, with a serious look on his face, said something that permanently affected my life. "Why are you walking like that?" I was stopped in my tracks, completely mortified. I didn't know how to respond. Something in my brain was triggered, and I instantly realized that something was recognizably different in me and that whatever it was, it must be wrong. I was old enough to comprehend what was happening at that moment but too young to know how to deal with it. I felt exposed yet I didn't know what or how to cover it up. I felt like I was caught for something that I had no idea that I was doing and couldn't necessarily help. Though this realization was a relief of sorts because I now knew I was indeed "different" and validated how I was feeling inside for as long as I could remember, it didn't make it any easier. I was now feeling vulnerable and utterly fearful of other people seeing the same thing my dad did and telling my Mom. I quickly changed the subject and tried my best to act 'normal.' My dad might've gotten the hint of what I was, but I wasn't ready for anyone else to make the same discovery. From that moment and for the next almost two decades of my life I would spend every second in my head over analyzing and critiquing everything I did to avoid being caught. The words my dad said to me that day planted a seed in my mind that with time continued to grow until it was a monster that took over tormenting me with my thoughts. I know that he didn't realize what he was saying would impact me in such a way or that it would affect me moving forward, but it did in a very profound way.

After that, I was never excited to see my dad. I didn't want to go with him at all. In fact, I avoided my dad at all costs. I never wanted to feel so exposed and uneasy again. I was nervous about being around him, afraid that he would figure out what I was and hate me for it. I felt like he was now on to me and that scared me greatly. It was the first time anyone had pointed out that they saw something different in me, and it made me feel so uncomfortable and shameful that I never wanted to experience that feeling again. This pivotal experience caused an invisible rift between my father and me, and consequently, our relationship suffered. As a result, I lost the connection with my siblings from his other marriages. The words that my dad told me that day became a part of me, etched

THE BRIDGE OF IDENTITY

on my spirit, like a tattoo I could not erase. I was marked. Even to this day, I catch myself reminding myself to walk "right" when I get out of the car or go in public. It comes so naturally that I don't realize I'm doing it.

I tried harder. I tried harder to walk the way the other boys walked, to talk the same way they did. I paid extra attention to what the other boys did and constantly compared how I did things to the way they did. If I had to get up to walk across the classroom, I'd pay attention to how I got up and walked. If I had to walk home, I'd pay attention to how I was walking and who was watching. If I had to talk to people, I'd pay attention to how I would talk. Everything was overanalyzed and critiqued, and I never shared what I was thinking with anyone, not even my Mom. The pressure that this placed on me as a child was so overwhelming and it only got worse with time, because it became a part of how I functioned and who I was. I was the boy who was deathly afraid of being caught and hurting his mom. That fear fueled this way of thinking until I had no control of it. Once you bring something to someone's attention, especially a child, how do you tell them to forget it? They won't forget. In fact, extra attention will be placed on it. It was as if a veil had been lifted in my mind of how I perceived myself and the world around me, and I didn't know what any of it meant, and it consumed me trying to figure it out. From that day forward, I became a master at pretending. Every mannerism was pre-calculated. I was no longer myself. A huge part of me was closed off and put inside a box, hidden away so no one could discover it. I lived in a self-imposed prison for my entire childhood and early adult years.

There's a strong sense of traditional manliness or 'machismo' that's rooted in Latin and Hispanic culture. Boys play with trucks. Girls play with dolls. That's how it goes in the Hispanic culture, with no questions asked. We don't get a choice. No one asks us if we want to be categorized in this sort of way. By being a man, we're automatically upheld to a certain level of masculinity that becomes the defining factor of just how much of a man we are and the level of our worthiness that dictates how much love and acceptance we'll be shown. Where did this leave me? Where did I fit in? Very early on, as a gay child, growing up sometimes seemed like a small seed, something that does not make sense, and having an attraction to the same sex seems normal. Soon, however, society and the world around you makes it abundantly clear that that attraction and that being gay is something you should be ashamed of, and something that is viewed as evil and wrong, from a religious perspective. That terrified me and I felt so alone.

THE BRIDGE OF IDENTITY

These were the concerns I would often worry about as a young child before I pushed the thought away.

One day, I went over to my friend's house to play, as I normally would. I was greeted by my friend's grandfather, who was outside smoking a cigar. He let me know my friend was not home. He asked me to come in to wait for him and have something to drink, and I did. After a few short minutes of waiting, he politely requested that I follow him to his bedroom. I didn't think anything of it. I knew him. Then he shut the bedroom door, and another side of my friend's grandfather appeared. It was a side I had never seen before in any person. He started fondling me, touching me underneath my clothes. I felt paralyzed and couldn't move but still, he grabbed my hand and made me do things to him. His body reeked with the stench of cigar smoke. A smell that to this day instantly takes me back to that home and it's unbearable. At six years old, my innocence was taken from me. Poof….gone- just like that. My once-innocent eyes saw the world for what it really was. I knew the secret that all adults were hiding. Even through the confusion, I knew what it all meant, but I didn't understand why I was included in it. So much of what happened is now a blurred, but what I remember most is the feeling it left me with and what he told me when he was done. He instilled guilt in me by telling me if I disclose the abuse there would be negative consequences for me. In retrospect, as an adult, I can now see that was his way of making me feel voiceless by exerting power and control over me. As I was leaving his room, the house now seemed dark and uninviting. I walked out of my friend's house and left with the feeling that there really was something wrong with me. I felt sick and unbalanced, like a piece of me was missing. It was a violation and it disturbed me to my core. Why did he choose me to do this to? Why didn't I stop it? I went home that day no longer an innocent child, and the shame this caused me coupled with the shame I already felt for being different was tremendous.

The immediate aftermath of the event left me feeling shocked and feeling a sense of helplessness, and a lot of guilt. It was forced upon me, and I was left with no option other than to repress it and deal with it the best I could. That's what I did. I swallowed my fear, my sadness, and my pain and put on my pretend face, the face that smiled and laughed and looked so innocent and happy. That was the face that I showed the world. I didn't do this just for myself. I did this also for her, my Mom. I never wanted to be the reason tears came out of her eyes. I never wanted to cause her stress or worry, because I witnessed all the stress she carried every day and I knew if I had told her this, it would only upset her. I knew what had been done couldn't be undone, so I dealt with it myself the best way I knew how- by being silent. I knew that if my Mom had the slightest doubt of my safety being jeopardized, she'd never forgive herself. I don't want people to think that my unfortunate event was in any way a reflection of my Mother as a parent, because it's not. I think it's so important to understand that parents can't be with their child 24/7, and sexual abuse can happen even within loving and protective families. My Mother can't be responsible for the actions of the abuser. Sexual abuse is the result of the abuser's choices and behaviors, and not mines or my Mother's. I knew that she nor anyone in my friend's family had any idea what that man was really about. I never stepped into that home ever again, even when my friend and his mother were home. I didn't come around as often as I used to and when I did, I would only play with my friend outside the house. His grandfather would watch us from the front porch, and I would feel his eyes on me, even from afar. To keep the peace, I went on with life and stuffed the truth away into the same dark corner where my other secret was, and I never spoke a word of it to anyone, until now. I found out a few years ago that this man had died, and I felt nothing. I've navigated through life with this secret for so long, but

THE BRIDGE OF IDENTITY

I never let it define me. Even though in a way he might've succeeded in silencing me, I now get to reclaim my voice by speaking my truth.

Unspoken secrets only grow with time, they don't go away or get better. As I got older, it seemed like no matter how hard I tried, kids always detected my "gayness," and they were ruthless about it. In middle school I was constantly bullied and shoved to the ground. They would do these limp wrists hand gestures to me because they knew I was gay. I never knew how to react or what to do, so I did what I do best- I stayed silent. By the time I started high school I realized my athletic skills and became very active in sports. As a result, I had a lot of friends that were boys. I'm sure this threw off any suspicions that my Mother would have of me because I was always doing "boy" activities. I dated a few girlfriends just for show, and the moment they wanted to be intimate or do anything sexual I would find an excuse or way out of it. The relationships never lasted long because of that. I had absolutely no interest in being intimate with any female but I knew I had to continue playing this game so I wouldn't be caught.

THE BRIDGE OF IDENTITY

When I was growing up, my Mom and I always lived in studio-like apartments called "efficiencies" that were usually connected in the back of a family home. For a working single mom, it was what she could afford at the time. Mom and I lived in these efficiencies and moved frequently from one efficiency to another. My Mom was always working tirelessly to provide and pay the bills, and the moment I came of age I immediately began applying for jobs so I could help her out. At sixteen years old, I got my very first part-time job with Walmart. Every time I got my check, I'd immediately give it to my Mom. If there was anything I needed for school, I'd take that out of my check to pay for it. I never wanted to bother her about any school-related expenses. With my part- time job, I was able to save enough money to buy my own school ring and cover any class trips, like Grad Night at Disney World. Especially during Senior Year when there were so many school activities leading to graduation. I never wanted my Mother to worry about any costs relating to school. I found a way to take care of it myself, because again, nothing was worth adding any stress to my Mom.

My secrets haunted me and by the time I had graduated high school and started college I had contemplated suicide several times. I thought about how I would do it and had decided on taking a whole bunch of pills and slowly just fade out of this world. I imagined the relief I'd feel of not having to spend another day with this monster in my head, pretending, and lying like I'm alright. I imagined meeting God and explaining to Him or She why I had to do it, and yes I feared God's wrath but more than fearing God, I feared what my death would do to my Mom. I feared hurting my Mom more than I feared upsetting God. The moment I thought of my Mom, the thought of killing myself was taken off the table and I had to muster up the courage to face another day, to get myself out of bed, and trudge on like it was all alright. I wasn't experiencing life at all. I was only existing and even that was on auto pilot. Quite often I would sink into deep depressions. My mood and entire energy would be very dark, and my Mom would always find a way to uplift me or get me out of it without even realizing that I was suffocating within and was knee-deep in feeling extreme anxiety and depression.

What's done in the dark, though, will always surface to the light, one way or another- one day. Although it felt like an endless struggle, that day did come later as a young adult. I had sunk into another depression, but this time it was different than the others. It wasn't brought on by loneliness but by love. I was 24-years old and had fallen

THE BRIDGE OF IDENTITY

in love the day before my birthday. I was sitting at home watching tv the night before my birthday and one of those cheesy after-hours hotline commercials came on. I never called any of these before even though I had seen them plenty of time. I don't know what it was about that night, but I decided to call in. Never having dated or even talked to another man, I decided to make my profile over the phone using an alias. After making a quick profile over the phone, I hung up thinking nothing of it, but moments later the operator called me and said there was someone on the other line who was a good match. I couldn't believe it, and honestly thought it was some type of joke. I figured I had nothing to lose and decided to entertain it. Surprisingly, me and this other guy had a lot in common and seemed to click. We wanted to meet that night, and I was beyond nervous. I knew it was dangerous meeting someone late at night that I didn't even know but just when I was ready to hang up on him, out of curiosity I asked him where he would want to meet. To my surprise he mentioned a location that was literally across the street from a place I used to work in. I thought it was such an unusual coincidence and something in me told me I needed to do this. My heart was pounding the whole ride there. When I parked the car, it was a little past midnight, and I saw this man walking towards me and I swear I thought I was being punked. He looked just like the vision I had always had of the perfect person for me. Everything about him. I was in complete disbelief and couldn't understand how this was real or even happening. I was very quiet and intimidated because I was so nervous and in shock. We decided to go to the beach to talk some more. I followed him there in my car, and on the way there he called my cell phone and asked if I was even interested in him. I realized I needed to shake off the nervousness and express myself because this man was exactly what I dreamt of. We spent the next five hours talking about our lives. It was absolutely insane how much we had in common. First, both of our last names were Suarez. He was also Cuban but was born here in the United States.

It felt like home being with him even though I had just met him. The only word to describe the experience was that it was magical. On the way home, I even wondered if I was in love. From that night forward, him and I were inseparable. We spoke every day and saw each other any chance we had. I knew that he was the person that I wanted to spend the rest of my life with but sense I had spent my entire life in this prison, silent, I had no way to express to anyone what I was feeling. Everything started to feel dark and hopeless for me.

THE BRIDGE OF IDENTITY

This voice in my head convinced me that it would be such a letdown for my Mother because I was her only son, and she would be very upset. She might cry or even worse shut me out or disown me. These thoughts replayed in my mind, and the only choice I could see was either death or live in silence my whole life which felt even worse. I was in the room, in the dark, and I knew that I had to tell her. There was no other choice because my mind could no longer live with the burden it was carrying. I called and told her we needed to talk, and she could hear the seriousness and desperation in my voice and immediately left work to come talk to me. I couldn't even get the words out. She started asking questions and I would nod my head no, until she asked if I was gay. I stalled. I felt paralyzed with fear, but I knew this was it. My throat was shut, and I couldn't physically speak. With every ounce of strength, I forced myself to nod yes. I was able to finally open up to the one person who means the absolute world to me and tell her my truth. She listened, she understood, and my pain instantly became her pain. We cried together. Telling my Mom the truth about my sexuality was a weight lifted off my shoulders. I felt a huge burden lifted from my spirit, and for the first time in my life, I experienced a cleansing of my heart, a relief that was indescribable. That moment was forever life changing. For the first time in my entire life, I was indeed one hundred percent liberated from the self-imposed prison I had adapted to for so long, a prison that provided me "comfort" and so much pain. I made the decision to stop running from what I perceived as a monster, and turned around and faced it and, more importantly, embraced it. In doing so, I realized that it was never a monster at all. It was only a small part of me that had been trying to catch up to me all this time. And in the light, it was beautiful. Ridding myself of the burden of carrying secrets brought me closer to my Mom in a way that I never thought was possible. I ended up marrying the man I met that night. As it turned out, I was right, it was love at first sight. My husband, Alberto, became my Mom's second son and she became his second Mother. We're family.

Looking back, I now understand that I should've never waited this long to tell her, but naturally, I was afraid of fear of rejection most of all. As a teen, I had heard my Mom one day having a conversation with a friend at a family get-together at our house and agreeing with the other person when they made a remark referring to homosexuality in a manner of disgust. I'm not entirely sure if she truly had those feelings or she simply agreed just to awkwardly brush off the conversation, but I remember thinking, "Oh my God. This is how she is going to feel about me." I allowed that one instance to further convince me that I couldn't tell her the truth. The thought of being rejected by the one person I loved the most was unbearable. The fear was so intense that it blinded me to what I knew to be true about my Mom's love and our indestructible bond as Mother and son. I should've known that her response would be what she has always shown me, nothing but unconditional love and acceptance. I should've trusted our connection. There is nothing that communication, understanding, and love can't solve. I think that having this compassion and grace for each other has helped me feel more at ease to continue to express my truth to my Mom so that she can understand me more as a person.

Mom and I almost died getting to America, six days on a raft in the ocean. Facing death together bonded us in a way no one can really understand unless experienced. To be forced as a parent to watch your son struggle to stay alive and not be able to do anything to help him puts life on a whole different perspective. Nothing else matters after that but knowing that your child is alive and well and that they will live to grow up. It was the same for me- I appreciated her even more after that experience. More than I could ever explain. It was that journey that created a bridge of what was to what will be, and all because of her sacrifice to get us there. Growing up, Mom

THE BRIDGE OF IDENTITY

was the person that saved me from dying inside, even when she didn't know it. She was always my reason why. In my eyes, her love deserved only the best.

CHAPTER 2

THE BURDEN OF A DREAM

"Twenty years from now, you will be more disappointed by the things you didn't do than by the ones you did. So throw off the bowlines. Sail away from the safe harbor. Catch the trade winds in your sails. Explore. Dream. Discover."

- Mark Twain

THE BURDEN OF A DREAM

Mom was a dreamer born in the wrong place at the wrong time in the world. A rebel since birth. She was born on May 30, 1953, in Cuba. Any dreamer was confined and restricted under Cuba's regime, and while most gave way to their dreams for more, my Mother remained optimistic that hers will one day come true. Many Cubans conformed to the limits the government placed on their speech and expression, but my Mom refused. She openly spoke about her feelings and thoughts when given the opportunity, even if sometimes it was only at home. Which isn't as easy as it sounds when her own mother championed everything my Mother was rebelling against. The older she got, it placed a lot of tension on the relationship she had with her, because my grandma fully supported the Cuban regime. During that time, the people that supported Castro were referred to as "Fidelistas," as they were die-hard Castro followers. They staunchly supported Fidel Castro's ideology, policies, and revolutionary ideals and often admired Castro's charismatic leadership, his ability to defy the United States, and his commitment to social equality and national sovereignty. They viewed Castro as a champion of the working class and the poor. Completely not realizing they were being brainwashed. Their unwavering loyalty to Castro and his vision for Cuba made them blindly defend his actions, downplay or dismiss criticisms of his government's human rights record, and reject any notions of political pluralism or liberal democracy. They even organize themselves into grassroots movements, participate in political rallies, and promote Castro's legacy through various means, like the CDR or Committees for the Defense of the Revolution, where they would promote social cohesion, monitor community activities, and safeguard the Cuban Revolution's principles and goals. Because they were organized at a local level, members would act as neighborhood watchdogs, reporting any suspicious activities or potential threats to the local authorities and maintain public order. Fidel Castro's charismatic personality and his ability to connect with people on an emotional level played a significant role in cultivating a cult of personality around him. It was fanaticism and caused strain on many families in Cuba, including the relationship between my grandma and Mom. Their relationship became a lot worse when I was born, because it was then that my Mother perceived the world differently. As a result, the nurturing and loving relationship that a mother and daughter are supposed to have shifted to one of severity and resentment.

THE BURDEN OF A DREAM

Regardless, Mom held the dream for a better life, even though everything around her didn't offer any hope for better, from the country's government to the conditions she lived in, to the mindset of everyone around her. From a very young age my Mother never felt like she belong in Cuba. Every picture of my Mother during her younger years in Cuba all show a sadness behind her eyes, every single one. The world around her was very narrow-minded, where exhibiting a different outlook was constantly judged and treated as an outcast. She couldn't help feeling a sense of inadequacy. She knew, deep in her heart, that Cuba was not the right place for her and all she wanted was to wake up each day in a place where she belong. My Mother grew up in extreme poverty. She was raised in a shack with a floor made of dirt and an outside latrine as the only bathroom for a family of eight. Although the shack was located in what was technically the city and not the country, her family still lacked the necessary resources to grow or create anything better for themselves. Yet, she still dared to dream of more.

She was the second oldest of six- all girls. As one of the oldest, she was expected to carry a lot of the responsibilities of caring for her siblings. It's always the responsibilities that are automatically expected of us that become our

THE BURDEN OF A DREAM

burden to carry through life, and it was no different for my Mother. It became impossible to attend school, care for her younger sisters, and earn money to help the household, so at fifteen years old, she decided to do what she thought was best and quit school, sacrificing her hopes for an education and putting the idea of a better life on hold for a more convenient time. Unfortunately, that more convenient time never seemed to come. While some of her family's conditions improved, like her dad putting cement on the floor of their home so that it was no longer bare dirt and also installing a working bathroom inside, their struggle still persisted. For Mom, it felt like settling for the scraps thrown their way, and adding to her frustration was that no one else saw it that way. Aside from being humble, my grandparents were also uneducated and extremely programmed by scarcity. It was what life was. Any other way of going about life that put into question how they lived was immediately shut down and frowned upon. My grandfather was very antiquated and what we call "bruto"- controlling. He didn't want any of his daughters to have goals for more or dream of anything other than being a wife and a mother one day. He didn't see women as equals but more as property that needed protection, and they needed to adhere to what he said they should do. Maybe that was the reason that my grandmother was so emotionally disconnected and cold from the time my Mother can remember. My Mom describes many of the older generation during that time in Cuba being like that. They weren't affectionate but would show their love through providing, making sure their children looked good, were fed, and cleaned. My grandpa would wake up every morning and make everyone breakfast; actions like that was how he expressed his love to his family. There were very little I love you's from them, and the few dear memories my Mother has of them are few and far between. Still, they're special to her. My Mom recalls the family not having money to celebrate special birthdays, like her "Quinces", her fifteenth birthday, which is similar to a Sweet Sixteen. Even so, her mother bought a special fabric to make a beautiful dress for my Mom to wear on her birthday. My Mom remembers feeling so special that day while wearing the beautiful handmade dress my grandma had made her. Poverty made all the little things so meaningful and memorable. She recalls the recession hitting Cuba and my grandfather being out of work. Consequently, he had to leave home a few days a week to work in another city in Cuba, and when he came back home, he'd always have a sack of groceries. My Mom and her sisters would be so ecstatic and would run to him at the door to greet him and see what goodies he had brought home. Many of it being things they couldn't find in town, like condensed milk and sugar. Before my Mom's younger sisters were born they lived in a small house that had a backyard, and my grandfather built a play house for my mom and her older sister. They played house for hours. To this day, every time Mom is at a department store and sees small kitchen gadgets, it instantly takes her back to that memory of playing pretend with her sister all those years ago. For an extended period, while Fidel Castro was in power, Cubans didn't celebrate Christmas, but instead, Three Kings Day on January 6th. My Mom remembers that no matter what my grandfather always made sure that something was given to each of his daughters. Once my Mom and her oldest sister found out that the gifts were from my grandparents and not the Three Kings, my grandfather would take them both with him to buy a gift for their younger siblings and while they were there, he would let my mom and her sister pick something for themselves. It was memories like these that my Mom tried to hold onto growing up while experiencing the change in the treatment from her parents as she grew older. Maybe my grandma, deep down, was frustrated and resentful because she was forced to shut out her own self and conform to her husband's needs and the government, and consequently, she shut everyone else out around her. For a rebel like my Mom, though, my grandparent's attempts to shut her down didn't sit well with her soul, and it proved to be a constant battle for them to silence her spirit.

My Mom had two main passions that sadly were never realized. She loved fashion. She would watch Spanish singer and actress Rocio Durcal in her 1960s films completely in awe and inspired by her progressive sense of style. My Mom and her friends would go to a neighborhood seamstress so they can duplicate some of the clothes they saw Rocio in. Mom's second passion was dancing. She felt the freest when she got to dance. She dreamt of being a dancer one day. Of course, that was frowned upon by her father. She'd only get the opportunity to dance in the rare occurrence of her own privacy, on the walk to school, or with the few friends that understood. My grandfather would catch her dancing while sweeping the floors and would beat her and tell her, "This can't be my daughter. She must've been switched at birth." He tried to shame her into silence. Even at a young age, she had no one to turn to for protection from his beatings or lashing of the tongue. She couldn't even turn to her Mother to validate her dreams or beautiful mind. She was forced to only turn to herself, and her spirit was so strong that despite all his attempts to kill her thoughts of dreaming for more

THE BURDEN OF A DREAM

were still not enough to dim her fire within. To him, it was nonsense that would eventually get her into trouble later in life. The thought of any of his daughters living in a modern world was not fathomable to him at all. He refused to even let them date even when they were young adults. Little did he understand that no matter what he did she wouldn't conform to him or the Cuban government for that matter. She absolutely refused. She continued to hold her desire and dream for a better life, one where she could freely express herself and have the chance to grow and create something meaningful. The older she got, the more she realized that the only way to do this was to leave. Her parents' belief system and father's overbearing rules stifled her, and the older she got the worse it was with him. Even if she decided to leave home and relocate somewhere else on the island, the country's government still made her feel trapped. Leaving Cuba was the only way. It was the only way to a new way of life. As time passed, my Mother's already strained relationship with her parents became more tense.

April 1, 1980, the headline news all over the world was about the diplomatic status of tens of thousands of Cuban citizens seeking asylum. Word quickly got out to the people of Cuba that six Cuban citizens had made their way to the Peruvian Embassy. A day later, 25 other citizens gatecrashed their way into the unguarded Embassy, and another day after that, 300 more. Every hour that passed, Cubans flooded the Embassy, ready to leave Cuba. Families with children of all ages fled in with nothing but hope in their hearts and the few belongings that they were able to grab quickly.

The Embassy stayed unguarded, and within a few days' time, hundred upon thousands of Cuban citizens poured in non-stop. With each passing day, it became apparent to the entire world that the people of Cuba were growing more and more discontent with the control of the government, and it was made even worse by the implementation of food rationing. People were tired. The turn of events at the Embassy sparked hope like wildfire, and for many, it suddenly became alive instead of a far- distanced dream. My Mom and her friends were near the site where all the commotion was at. They saw a crowd running towards the Embassy, and with no hesitation, at a whim's notice, they ran with the group at what they believed was their only opportunity for a new life and joined the thousands of other citizens in Havana, Cuba. By April 6th, 10,865 Cuban citizens flooded the gates into the 2,000 square meter space of the Peruvian Embassy in Havana, Cuba, and were granted political protection by the Peruvian Ambassador,

THE BURDEN OF A DREAM

Ernesto Pinto Bazurco Rittler, who had come upon an agreement with Castro to label them "migrating people" instead of asylum seekers or refugees. Unfortunately, the gates were closed when my Mom and her friends arrived, yet in one last desperate attempt, they boldly joined the others, pleading and screaming at the top of their lungs for diplomatic protection from the Peruvian government. Despite Fidel Castro having issued a warning just days prior that any Cuban citizen storming the Embassy would lose their right to safely depart Cuba, my Mom stood her ground and risked it all. Shortly after, the police ended up coming to de-escalate the chaos that was taking place and disperse the people to go home. Many were beaten by police.

With all eyes on Cuba, it was quickly becoming an embarrassment to the government that their people were clearly unhappy and willing to risk it all to leave. They started building barricades to block the entrance to the Embassy, further fueling the crowd of people there protesting and crying out for help. From my Mom's group of friends, she was one of the few that got arrested. Thankfully, by then, Castro had retracted his latest threat to de-escalate tensions and agreed to give any citizen arrested or caught storming the Embassy a green "safe-conduct" pass, allowing them to go home without any further consequence.

My Mom was released home by early morning, and to her surprise, her dad had no clue as to what happened to her. If he did, he'd probably have beaten her. My Mom endured physical abuse from her dad well into her adult years, even after she moved out of his house. To make matters worse, her relationship with my grandma had become even more strained throughout the years all mostly due to the pressure from the regime of Fidel Castro. My grandmother continued to support Castro heavily, and with my Mom being the exact opposite of her, the rift between them was evident. They never saw eye to eye. It became even more of a reason to my Mom that there was nothing for her in Cuba. The Peruvian Embassy crisis ended up being a disaster. Those who got past the gates were left on the embassy grounds for weeks with deplorable conditions in man-made tents from things they found nearby and had to endure rain and scorching heat. Without much to eat, some say people were starving and were forced to eat leaves from the trees on the embassy grounds. Ultimately, my Mom was glad she didn't end up leaving thru the Peruvian Embassy. However, she kept her hope alive and jumped on any opportunity to escape. That opportunity came just two weeks after the crisis at the Peruvian Embassy when Fidel Castro announced that any Cuban citizen was free to leave the country if they wanted. The tension and restlessness that started amongst the people could not be taken away, and the Cuban government most likely recognized that unless they gave them a "way out," people would start banding together to fight back, which would result in a civil war. Negotiations between Cuba and the U.S. governments took place, and a deal was struck that allowed Cubans to leave the country legally by boat from the port of Mariel, located west of Havana. At first, the agreement stipulated that the U.S. would admit over 3,000 Cubans under the Refugee Act of 1980, the final number exiles ended up being much larger. Hundreds of thousands of Cuban citizens headed to the Mariel Harbor in search of a boat to leave the country for the United States. Families once again were willing to risk everything, including their children's lives at sea in small boats and overcrowded vessels, to make it to the land of opportunity. 125,000 Cubans left on boats to the United States in a span of six months; this exodus of Cubans became known as the "Mariel Boatlift," and my Mom was determined not to miss her chance. She would often go to the Mariel Harbor looking for a boat, scanning the shores to see if there was anybody that could possibly help. To her detriment, there were none. Each time she was left with no other choice but to go back home to what seemed like a prison sentence.

As time progressed, people started to learn the way the Mariel Boatlift worked. Many of the migrants that were allowed to leave were a mixture of bona fide political prisoners while the rest were other Cubans seeking better economic opportunities getting special preference if they had family members who were already in the United States and were able to claim them. However, Castro used this opportunity to forcefully discard convicted criminals, insane asylum patients, LGTBQ people, and prostitutes out of the island and into the boats, who he crudely labeled as "escoria" or trash. There were also horrible things done to people that were selected to leave. The Cuban government organized mobs to viciously attack those who chose to leave, as an act of repudiation. The mobs would express their disdain by surrounding their targets and scream out vulgarities to them, force them to wear accusatory signs around their necks, beat and ridicule them on the streets of their neighborhoods. My Mom recounts one specific incident, that to this day, brings tears to her eyes. One of her co-workers was lucky enough to have a relative come get her during the boatlift. On the day her co-worker was filing the discharge paperwork at work, the company made it a point to get every employee to stop working, block the entrance with guards so no one could leave, lined everyone up outside of the HR office and waited for the lady to walk out of the office. The moment the lady stepped out they made employees shame her by yelling out vulgarities, calling her names, and throwing things at her. My Mother refused to participate. She stood there motionless with tears slowly rolling down her face as the humiliation took place.

The influx of Cuban migrants from the Mariel Boatlift presented challenges for the United States. The sudden arrival of a large number of people overwhelmed U.S. immigration facilities, and the migrants faced varying reactions from American society, including discrimination. Some communities and organizations welcomed the Cubans and provided support, while others expressed concerns about the potential impact on the economy and social services. The arrival of the "Marielitos," as the migrants came to be known, had social and political implications, and led to changes in U.S. immigration policies. In Cuba, the departure of a significant number of people, including professionals and skilled workers, had an impact on the country's economy and social structure. The Mariel Boatlift remains a significant event in the

THE BURDEN OF A DREAM

history of both Cuba and the United States, highlighting the challenges and complexities of migration and political asylum.

As each year passed and nothing changed for the better, the morale and spirit of the people throughout Cuba were at an all-time low, and social tension was on the rise. The misery of the people was like a thick fog from which there was no escape. There was a severe recession, food was being rationed by the government, and able bodies that could work didn't have work or were not mentally capable of working because of depression. Resentment and anger mounted and grew inside everyone, showing themselves in different ways. My Mom hated her life in Cuba, and her recollection of many memories is foggy and broken. She believes that this was her brain's defense mechanism in dealing with all the trauma- to forget. When each day carries its own burden to survive, often the load becomes too much to bear, and there is no other choice for us to survive but to numb ourselves and mentally check out and move on autopilot. It wasn't an ideal time for anyone, but most especially for a young woman to be pregnant and start a family. It was hard enough just surviving. My Mom's dreams never included her being married or settling down

THE BURDEN OF A DREAM

with a man, but her heart always yearned to be a mother one day. She longed to feel the weight of a baby in her arms.

My parents met through friends, and it was one of those casual on-and-off relationships. They began a secret romance that no one knew about during the early stages. It turned out my dad was in a serious relationship with another woman, and my Mom didn't realize it at first. One day, my dad came into town with his significant other, and my Mom happened to see them together at his mother's home. She realized then that she was the other woman. Despite this, their secret affair continued thereafter. My Mom had blindly fallen in love with him. Their relationship was, for the most part, one-sided, as she was really interested in my dad and obviously more emotionally invested, and he wasn't. A couple of years passed, and at twenty-nine, my Mom found out she was pregnant, and immediately after, their relationship ended. My dad wanted no part in the pregnancy. He didn't want the responsibility of having another child since he was in a serious relationship with his then- spouse, and they already had a son of their own at this point, my oldest brother.

THE BURDEN OF A DREAM

My Mom knew what her parents' reaction would be, so she hid her pregnancy until she couldn't anymore. When the time came for her to confess the truth that was so obvious by her growing belly, they reacted exactly how she had expected. They were upset with her, and needless to say, my grandfather's outdated mindset caused him to feel ashamed that she would get pregnant outside of marriage and bring that kind of embarrassment to the family. He told her to leave. My grandmother remained silent to his demands, like always, and my Mom was left with no choice but to move into the only place she could afford- a hole in the wall. She did her best to make it on her own, and although it was difficult as a single pregnant woman, she was determined because, to her, I was that new beginning that her heart yearned for.

Sometimes I think about the heartache my mom felt while she was pregnant with me, the struggles she went through doing it all alone. Not only the physical strain from the lack of support, but the mental and emotional stress. Even though she never once said it out loud, I know from the minimal moments I've spoken to my Mom about this, that she would've loved for things to have been different. But that is not her story. The moment my Mother learned she was pregnant with me, she gain the inspiration she needed

THE BURDEN OF A DREAM

to take full control of her life and flourish in ways she never knew she could. Moms are such immense forces of nature. As I grew inside of her, it gave my Mother a profound new sense of purpose. A mother's purpose.

I was born on October 12, 1982, as Jalyll Hernandez. Growing up, I used to always hate my name because it was so different, and everyone always had a hard time pronouncing it and spelling it. My name would always require further explanation when meeting people, and I hated that. The thought of having to say my name out loud irked me beyond belief. My Mom loved my name though. When she gave birth to me, she hadn't come up with a name yet. She remembered this man that her friend dated that was named, Jalyll, and she remembered how much she liked that name. I suppose it is fitting, and with time I've learned to love my name because just like my name, my life has been different. Similar to pronouncing my name, you won't be able to understand me without trying a few times.

My dad never came to the hospital. In fact, it wasn't until I turned three that he gave me his last name and owned on paper that he was my father. My Mother warned him that if he was to give me his last name, he needed to do it before

THE BURDEN OF A DREAM

I began school. She didn't want me to face the inevitable judgement from other kids at school. However, his main change of heart decision was influenced mostly by my father's mother, my grandmother. It didn't surprise me to have learned that when I was older. My grandmother had such a beautiful aura. I loved the feeling of being around her. Her presence was warm, and she always did things that made me feel loved. She would grab my hands and gently massage them as she talked to me about life. She would gaze deep into my eyes and was genuinely interested in things I had to say. My dad's personality was the opposite of hers, he was more reserved, he didn't express himself much to me and came across as cold. At three years old, I officially became Jalyll Suarez. This sparked a huge argument between my grandfather and Mom because my grandfather didn't want me to have my father's last name. In his eyes, it was too late, and at that point, he felt my dad didn't deserve to be registered as my father. My Mom argued, though, that I would resent my father later in life if I didn't have my own father's last name, so my grandfather agreed, and my last name was changed to my father's even though he was still more like a stranger to me at the time. Again, with the push of his mother, my father reached out to my Mother asking her if she needed him to provide child support for me, to which my mom responded with a

THE BURDEN OF A DREAM

"no". After the fiasco of getting him to legally register me, she was so hurt by everything that transpired, that she was determined to do it on her own. From the beginning of my life, it was always just us- my Mom and me.

CHAPTER 3

UNDER ONE RULER

"The most effective way to destroy people is to deny and obliterate their own understanding of their history."

- George Orwell

UNDER ONE RULER

How do people of a country slowly lose their voice and human rights? How does a man like Fidel Castro just assume power over an entire nation? How was it that he went from being a political activist to becoming a Communist dictator? They say history repeats itself until the lesson is learned, and I really believe that is true because so many have forgotten what it was like, or their sense of what is true has been contorted through media. Knowing my country's history has always given me an extra awareness of what I believe from the media and government because I know that's how it all starts- the manipulation of people through media. That's how it began for my country with Castro.

Before Castro came into power, the former President of Cuba was a man named Fulgencio Batista. His administration was just as corrupt, but only in a different way. Even though one-third of the country was in poverty, his administration claimed that Cuba was one of the most developed countries in the region. His prominent supporters consisted of corrupt politicians and military officials, and the United States government supported him. Before he was overthrown by Castro during the Cuban Revolution, the Americans treated Cuba like it was their property. The 45-square mile U.S. Navy base at

Guantanamo Bay has been continuously occupied there since 1903. There was a flurry of casinos and brothels all over the country that was run by American gangsters. It was the go-to place for honeymooners and vacationers. The "sin island," as it was known, was a place for flings, sprees, and binges with a reputation as an exotic and permissive playground.

It wasn't a country that was taken seriously by the Americans. The United States withdrew support for Batista when Castro started to expose his corruption, greed, and brutality to the world. The United States didn't want to be associated with Batista's ways, but it was almost impossible to deny their associations when Castro and the group he led to overthrow Batista, called the 26th of July Movement, continued to work their tactic of using the media to reveal to the world the truth. The United States quickly sought other leaders besides Castro because they viewed him as a threat, but they weren't quick enough. Castro was able to gain the trust of the Cuban people during the revolution through propaganda. He did this by agreeing to personal interviews with journalists, radio broadcasts, and publicly seeking operations that contributed significantly to the victory of the rebels over Batista.

UNDER ONE RULER

Before the United States could stop him, Castro swooped in and successfully overthrew Batista. On January 1, 1959, all the Cuban people celebrated in Havana, the capital of Cuba, while Batista was forced to leave his country and fled to the Dominican Republic. Many of the Cuban people at the time felt that this was a win for the country because Castro's values seemed to be aligned with family values, hard work, and integrity, which meant that the country would be done being the world's playground hosting casinos and prostitution. The United States and the American people didn't anticipate this happening and were caught off guard, much like parents that watch their quiet child rebel. His defiance against the U.S. government and ability to resist multiple attempts to overthrow his regime solidified his image as a symbol of resistance against foreign intervention. This made him popular among anti-imperialist movements and leaders across the globe. Castro declared the island a socialist country and allied Cuba with the Soviet Union.

The United States immediately severed all diplomatic and economic ties with Cuba and enacted a trade and travel embargo that is still in effect today, although the rules have loosed a bit since the Obama administration.

UNDER ONE RULER

The American sanctions placed a heavy burden on the Cuban population, and as a result, food rationing amongst the people was implemented. In 1961, the United States then planned a secret assassination of Castro through an invasion called, The Bay of Pigs Invasion. It was obviously unsuccessful, and in response to these threats, Castro deepened his connection with the Soviet Union, whose relationship with the United States was already frail. Castro agreed to allow the Soviet Union to place nuclear weapons on the shore of Cuba so that Cuba could respond to any future attacks by the United States. President John F. Kennedy set a naval quarantine blocking any further missiles from reaching Cuba and demanded that all weapons of destruction be immediately dismantled. After several long days of tension, a negotiation was reached publicly, and Castro agreed to have the missiles dismantled. However, this resulted in what is now known as the Cuban Missile Crisis, and life in Cuba for the people has never been the same. Castro used this situation to vilify the United States to the Cuban people perpetrated by the media. The people slowly allowed their rights to be taken away, and before they realized it, they were under complete control of Castro's administration. Some of the abusive tactics he developed and used were to keep the people repressed and under his control with surveillance, beatings, arbitrary detention, and publicly denying the truth and their position on issues to cause confusion amongst the people. Many were executed through the application of the death penalty after trials that didn't meet the standard of due process. And thousands of people were sent to prison for many years for crimes of dissent opinions, public disorder, resistance, and assembly and remained in there for many years, with some never seeing freedom. While Castro argued that these measures were necessary to safeguard the revolution and protect Cuban power, they drew criticism from human rights organizations and governments worldwide.

In the 1980s, Cuba's economy was in a significant decline, and by the time the Soviet Union was disassemble, Cuba found itself without the help of its main ally. The result was devastating for the island, both economically and socially. Cuba has never recovered since. Traveling to Cuba today is like traveling back in time. As if time stood still. Castro's ripple effect of decades of damage is visible everywhere. Hardship, frustration, and disillusionment can be seen on the faces of the Cuban people. Major cities like Havana have suffered from years of neglect and decay. This once beautiful city by the sea finds itself with crumbling buildings; some have collapsed into piles of rubble. With so few resources, Cubans have adapted the ability to make do with so little. The dire circumstances have inherently made them some of the most ingenious and persistent people. I have so much of that in me, myself. Cuba did make improvements, and Fidel spearheaded enormous advances in health care, education, and literacy, but many of these gains were undermined by extended periods of economic hardship and by repressive policies.

Fidel Castro remained one of the longest leaders to ever be in power. Some perceive his leadership as the beginning of the rise of Cuba, and others see it as the fall of Cuba, but it depends on who you ask; some people can see through the smoke, while others just aren't able to. Castro's influence extended beyond Cuba's borders. He played a crucial role in supporting and fostering revolutionary movements in various countries, particularly in Latin America and Africa. Cuba provided military and ideological support to nations such as Angola, Mozambique, and Nicaragua, aiding them in their struggles against colonialism and imperialism. Castro's efforts to export the Cuban Revolution and promote socialist ideals influenced political dynamics in many regions. Castro's legacy is also tied to the process of succession and the transition of power in Cuba. After health issues forced him to step down as president in 2008, his brother Raúl Castro assumed leadership. This marked a significant transition in Cuba's governance, with limited reforms introduced to address economic challenges. The transition from Fidel to Raúl Castro, and subsequently to Miguel Díaz-Canel in 2018, signaled the end of an era and raised questions about the future trajectory of Cuban socialism, that is still unravelling.

Fidel died in 2016, but his polarizing figure is still felt and continues to influence Cuban society significantly. The state continues to rule with a heavy hand. There is still a lack of basic human rights and there is still no free press. At present, activists continue to face arrest and harassment for speaking out against the government. It is this repression of free speech that is Fidel Castro's darkest legacy. A legacy that is multifaceted and continues to elicit diverse perspectives. While he is celebrated by some as a champion of social justice, anti-imperialism, and national independence, his leadership style and human rights record remain a contentious topic.

Unfortunately, oppression takes new forms in Cuba today, and the country maintains a firm grip on almost every aspect of Cubans' lives. Cuba is naturally a fascinating and beautiful island, but paradise it ain't.

CHAPTER 4

CHAINED TO THE ISLAND

"Stop being a prisoner of your past. Become the architect of your future."

- Robin Sharma

CHAINED TO THE ISLAND

I imagine when a woman becomes pregnant unexpectedly, she still holds an expectation that the father will fulfill his roles and duties as the other parent, even if he doesn't want the pregnancy. I imagine when the father isn't supportive during the pregnancy, that a woman still carries hope in her heart that once the baby is born and he sees the baby, he will change. I'm sure when neither happens, there is sadness, anger, and overwhelming fear that she must deal with while being the sole parent of a newborn child. My Mother experienced all of it while not having the support of her own parents, especially from her father, in a country that controlled everything down to how much food she could purchase. After my Mom gave birth to me, my grandmother, on my father's side, helped my Mom get a place to live near her home on the same property. It was a tiny hole in the wall, yet my Mother was grateful because it was still a roof over our heads, a place where she felt free to make it work on her own without the stress of her parents dictating her every move. Still, my Mother's mental health and faith was tested. She was sleep deprived, didn't have a strong support system around her and was economically vulnerable. As a way to cope with all the stress, my Mom decided to abruptly chop her waist-length beautiful black hair, a transition that was symbolically representing what she was going through at the time.

My dad had not visited nor asked her about me. I was already a little over a month old. One day he showed up in town and walked past my Mother and me on the way to see his mother. He didn't say one word to my Mother, even though he knew we lived there. To add salt to the wound, he didn't ask to see me or to hold me- nothing. My maternal grandmother came to visit us and saw that my father was at his Mother's house, just a few yards from where we were. She refused to tolerate such a disgrace, so she took me from my Mother's arms, walked towards him and placed me in his arms, and said, "This is your son." I'm not sure if he held me for long or what he said, if anything at all, but I was just a few weeks old when he finally saw my face for the first time. It took him another three years to acknowledge me as his son and sign my birth certificate. Yes, with time, he came around. Still, the truth is the truth, and at the beginning of my life, my Mom was all I had and knew, and she experienced a lot of pain and sadness bringing me into this world.

From the time I was a baby to about four years old I suffered a lot with asthma. My mom was constantly in and out of the hospital with me because I was so sick. I'm sure my dad knew about all these visits, but he never offered to help or came with us. I saw pictures of my mom during this time, and she was so skinny from stress and not eating properly. She fought silent battles alone with me with nothing but her faith to lean on, but we made it through. By the time my dad did come into my life, my Mom was so strong from all that she persevered through that she was alright with or without him around. She didn't have time for any regrets but rather was driven to make the most of what was now her life as a mother.

I hated being an only child. I yearned to have a brother or sister close to me to play with every day, but I was thankful for having a lot of cousins in Cuba while growing up. I was lucky to have a brother and sister from my dad's side, but unfortunately, they lived in another province. The distance was always a factor in me getting to know them better. But the short moments I did have with them both, I treasure dearly. I recall holding my little sister's hand, walking around my grandma's house yard, and taking her to go see my Mom. She was younger than me, and even though I was a child myself, I felt protective over her. I also remember walking on the beaches of Varadero, where my dad worked, with my dad and brother. My brother would tease me when my dad wasn't looking. I was that annoying younger brother that would mimic everything he did. He was a few years older than me, and naturally, I wanted to be like him. But also, I was a little envious of him. Primarily because of his connection to my father, something I craved secretly. When we were together, I always witnessed their special bond, always on display.

Even more so, I realized how much I looked up to my dad, that is until I just didn't. Our interactions were few and far between, kind of sad considering I was still in Cuba. Thus, our relationship faded as more time passed between us, and as a result, my relationship grew stronger with my Mom. She was all I really cared about. She was all that mattered to me. Kids really do notice everything, even when you don't think they do. I don't think my Mom thought that I was watching everything she did, but I was. I was a highly intuitive child. I noticed the long hours she worked, which didn't stop once she got home. She then would have to juggle motherhood duties at home. I observed how she would come home exhausted but still ran around our small home, cooking and preparing meals, tackle essential household chores like cleaning and doing laundry by hand, helped me with homework when I needed it, and assist me with bathing and bedtime routines, the list goes on and on. My Mother made it a priority to implement a chip of wisdom in me very early on. She instilled the importance and impact of education. By the time I was two, I already knew how to count past 10, named many colors, knew animal names and the sounds they make and recited the national anthem of Cuba word for word. I remember all the camping trips she took me on around Cuba as our vacation. Magical places like "Puerto Escondido" were one of our favorite places to visit, a hidden beach paradise with crystal blue waters and spectacular coastal hills where we would cliff dive together. I remember all our weekend visits to the beach just to get away. I remember her sitting on the sand, watching me play in the ocean. We would stay on the beach all day, from early morning till sundown. It was her favorite pastime and so it became mine. That's where my love for the ocean began. It was one of the few times that her face looked like she had peace and happiness. It was so opposite from the look on her face that I was used to seeing throughout the week, especially when we had to wait in line to get our food.

The strict food rationing system that was in place, where families were assigned a certain amount of food for purchase, was such an infuriating process. Her face was one of frustration, disgust, and sadness that this was the reality she was raising me in. I vividly recall an incident that really was a defining moment between my Mother and grandmother. Citizens were forced to survive only on what the government chose to or could give them, even though there were times were there weren't certain foods to be issued at all. Or even worse, if the food happened to be spoiled or was rotten, they will still give it to you like that, just because they could. One day, when my Mother received her assigned liter of milk, she discovered it was spoiled. She pleaded with the distributors at the local bodega for a fresh one, but her cries fell upon deaf ears. Their apathy bothered my Mother, who stood there with me by her side. Out of frustration, she took the glass of spoiled milk and threw it against the ground, followed by a series of obscenities that shocked the others in the line. Without hesitation, my Mother spewed vulgarities against the government and Fidel Castro, to the surprise of many, especially my grandmother, who stood in line too, only a few people behind us. My grandmother yelled at my Mom to be quiet, silencing my Mother and telling her to return home. After a heated exchange between the two, my Mom and I left. My Mother understood at that moment that my grandmother would always choose to support the communist regime even over her own family. Her loyalty to the government came first, and it was her extremist ways that contributed to the wedge put in between her relationship with my Mom. The strain between the two was already real, but more so that day.

Everywhere you walked, everyone's face looked strained. So many citizens were exhausted, struggling to put food on their tables. The fall of the Soviet Union hit Cuba hard, and the island suffered great economic crisis. It was felt everywhere, a thick cloud of despair covered us with no ray of sunlight in sight. The energy was so serious. To make matters worse, there were people that used to get paid by the government to spy on people and report back to them who were acting out and rebelling against the government; because of this, everyone had to be very careful about anything they did and spoke. If twisted and misconstrued by the wrong person, it could cost you and your family a lot- often the little freedom you had left.

To add to the tension in our life, the relationship my Mom had with my grandpa also grew more difficult as I got older. Mom and I ended up moving in with my grandparents back in the home she grew up in. We outgrew the tiny place we were in when I was first born and my Mother couldn't find a place she could afford. She didn't have any other choice but to move in with my grandparents. Because my grandfather ran his home, he sort of gained control of my Mother again. Something she did not miss one bit. My grandfather, in essence, became my main father figure and was actively engaged in my life. He was extremely fond of me and overprotective. I am not sure what it was that made my grandfather act the way he was acting when it came to me and my Mother. Maybe it was the way he witnessed how I was conceived and that made him feel like he needed to protect us, but he went about it completely wrong. He would constantly shield me from any situation. He couldn't tolerate seeing my Mother disciplining me when I did something wrong and would go against her when she was reprimanding me. It became toxic and overbearing, a constant push and pull.

My Mother was able to find a place that she could afford in the same neighborhood. This is the place that I am most connected to, and truly felt like it was our first home. It was a small place, like a stand-alone square studio apartment, with a tiny bathroom. Mom and I slept on a twin-size bed, but it was good enough for both of us and we were happy. As an added bonus, our place was just a few yards from my cousin's house, who was the same age as me. I have so many fond memories of us playing for hours, climbing massive tamarind trees, getting in the dirty river and we have the scars to prove it.

Even though we were already settled in and living on our own, my grandfather would still show up regularly, almost daily as if he thought he could exert control. He would be the one to take me to school and pick me up, which did help my Mother in that aspect. But he wanted to control my Mother's every move. We were no longer living with him, nor did he financially support us, yet he felt entitled to say how my Mom would discipline and raise me. I remember him coming over to our home one day, yelling at my Mom, and even slapping her; a grown woman, a single mother being abused in her own home by her father. Once again, I felt so helpless. On the outside, I was a small child, but on the inside, I felt like I was a grown man. How I wished I could fast forward time and be an adult already and shield my Mom to protect her. How I wish I could do all the duties and take all the problems away that I saw her dealing with every day. I knew, even then, that I couldn't, and all I could do was watch and be there for her. What made me even sadder was after my grandpa left, she'd put her strong face on for me. She wouldn't cry. She wouldn't make a fuss, and I knew that was for me. She was so used to abusive treatment that a part of her was desensitized to it all, and she had trained herself to shut it out and keep on going. Still, I knew she deserved better. I got an inside view of all that she did every day to survive and to try her hardest to give me a better life despite our limiting conditions. My Mom was breaking generational cycles without even fully being aware of it, and maybe that's why everything became so hard for her to accomplish and do. Anyone who is breaking generational cycles, I think, can understand, and relate that there is always a constant energy working against you when you're trying your best to do different, to shift the needle even a little in your and your children's life. When all odds, even the government, are working against you, it requires a level of tenacity and resilience that only a person being supported spiritually has. Life was hard, but my Mom was determined to make it better.

Even though I saw my grandpa mistreat my Mom because of his closed mindset and antiquated ways, I was sympathetic towards him. He had a good heart and deep down he really did mean well. He wanted what was best for me. I remember him going out of his way to spend time with me. He'd walk me to and from school, carrying my yellow backpack in one hand. I remember it so clearly. When he'd walk me home from school, he'd ask about my day and would always seem very interested in everything I had to say as I eagerly rambled on about all that I learned that day. I remember him making me feel heard and special.

By the late '80s through the early '90s, following the collapse of the Soviet Union and its severe impact on the island, many Cubans resorted to desperate measures to leave the country. There were other factors, however, beyond that of just the economic hardships that led to such measures, including political ideology, which shaped the landscape of the island and people were very much over it. These events had contributed to the desperation and desire for change among many Cubans, leading to the emergence of the "balsero" phenomenon as a means of escape. As a result, it had become prevalent to escape Cuba through self-made vessels known as "balsas" or rafts. Since Cuba is an island, the only way out was by sea and embarking on such journey is fraught with numerous challenges and perils. It was known throughout the island, but anyone willing to attempt such an escape knew they had to keep it under extreme secrecy. Getting caught resulted in prison time, and if, by any chance, someone was found with a child, it meant even more severe punishment.

One day in April of 1991, a man by the name of Jesus, who was the stepfather of a friend of my Mother's, came over to our house and asked my Mom if she knew of anyone who might be selling a motor. Immediately, my Mom boldly asked if it was to escape the island. At first, he hesitated to tell her the truth or give her any details of what it was for, but my Mom insisted, and finally, he told her that it was indeed to leave the country. My Mom begged him to take us with him. He immediately said no for the sole reason that I, a child, would be going. Not many were willing to take such risks with a small child. After much back and forth, my Mom told him she would do anything she could to find a motor for him as long as he would take us both with him. He begrudgingly accepted. They kept their meeting a secret, and for most of the month of April, my Mother cautiously went around town asking folks if they would sell her any small motor. Neither he nor my Mother ever found an engine. Jesus ended up pivoting his initial plan, and a few days later, my Mom received word from him to meet at a specific location on April 30, a Tuesday.

I went to school that day, hand in hand with my grandfather and my yellow school backpack like so many days before it. Nothing about that day felt different except for the way I was feeling while I was in school. I remember feeling restless and wanting to be home. Finally, school came to a close for the day and as I walked out looking for my grandfather, I instead saw my Mother waiting for me. I was happy to see her, but I thought it was odd because she was usually still at work at that time. Also, her demeanor felt different, as if she was hiding something from me. I kept my detection to myself, however. I didn't even ask her why she was picking me up and not grandpa, instead I went on and on rambling to her about what I learned that day. I was also eager to get home, eat a snack, and go outside to play with the other kids in the neighborhood like I always did. I had no clue that my life was about to change forever.

When we got home, before I could even take my school uniform off, my Mom sat me on the bed in our tiny home and asked me a very odd question. She looked straight into my eyes and asked me if I wanted to see my aunts and uncles who lived in the United States. My response was very enthusiastic "Yes!". At eight years old, the thought of being in the United States was a big deal. I had heard tales of the U.S. being a fantastic futuristic world where machines would do laundry for you and even the existence of fast cars. My imaginative young mind always pictured lots of lights everywhere with flying cars all around. So, of course, when my Mom made that proposition, it was hard to say no. Once I was all in, my Mom felt reassured and got the validation she was looking for to follow through with it. She then told me we were going to go on a trip to the United States. For some reason, I thought this trip would be like one of our camping trips. Boy, was I wrong.

She had me changed from my school clothes and grabbed a tiny little bag that she had packed, with only a few items like a small round deflated tube floaty for me, a small blanket, and a few cans of food. I would have never imagined that this was all that we'd leave for the United States with, especially in the manner that she had planned for us to escape. It never crossed my mind as we walked outside, leaving our house, that it would be the last time I would see the only place I ever called home. I also didn't realize at that moment that I would be leaving my whole family behind. My aunts and cousins who I was so close with, my friends, everyone. By this time, my grandfather was displaying signs of Alzheimer's and when he was told we had left it was another hit to his already deteriorating mental health. Later I learned that he would show up to my school with my yellow backpack with him, waiting for me by the entrance to take me home. Something that to this day brings tears to my eyes. I never got to officially tell him goodbye. He passed away five years later in 1996. Yet, these are things I didn't think about as a child when I was leaving and there was no way my Mom could've have done it any other way if she wanted us to have a real chance at escaping.

To leave our neighborhood, we had to go through the main street in our town, where all the neighborhood kids would gather to play after school. This was prior to any technology or video games, at least during a time that they weren't available in Cuba. I remember my Mom telling me that once we walk out, we must not talk to anyone or mention anything of what she just said to me at home. As we walked through the crowd of neighbors, my Mom's older sister saw her and jokingly said, "Make sure to send me a telegram." Perhaps, intuitively she knew. Once we got to the end of the main road, we boarded a bus and headed to our neighboring city, Santa Fe.

My Mom looked out the window, anxious and careful not to miss our exit. I had no idea what the plan was or where we were going. I was just excited to be going on an adventure with my Mom, and out of all places- to the United States! I reveled in my excitement and allowed the anticipation of it all to unfold itself to me as it came. I guess trusting the process, and releasing control, is part of the purity of a child that we forget as an adult.

Once off the bus, we walked for a little while along the coastline until we reached a house that was right on the water. The back of the house had a boat garage that led to the ocean, and there was a raft in the garage instead of a boat. I still didn't realize that this was what we'd be going to America on. There was still daylight left, and the others that would be joining us had yet to arrive. We were set to leave at night, to remain inconspicuous as possible. I listened with complete trust and faith in my Mom as she explained to me what we were about to embark upon. I could tell from her tone of voice and the way my mom was talking to me that she had a sense of good anxiety. In exchange, her calm tone made feel like something exciting was ahead. Even though I was paying close attention to what she was telling me, I was more captivated by the majestic tide pools a few steps away from the home we were in. As soon as my mom was done talking to me, she let me go off to play in these natural pools of ocean water before the sun went down. I ran off carefree, still full of enthusiasm. I always felt a deep connection with the ocean. It was a place of peace, one that brings up all my happy memories made with my Mom throughout my childhood. It made me feel safe and comfortable, like I was home. The sun twinkled on the water, inviting me to swim and play like I always had- so deceiving. Little did I know that the

CHAINED TO THE ISLAND

same place that I had so much love for would be the same place that would try to swallow us alive.

CHAPTER 5

WET FEET

"The Chinese use two brush strokes to write the word' crisis.' one brush stroke stands for danger, the other for opportunity. In a crisis, be aware of the danger-- but recognize the opportunity."

- John F. Kennedy

WET FEET

News travels fast in the small towns of Cuba and inquiring minds want to know. It didn't take long for someone to leak out our secret. A nearby neighbor had heard the news that we were embarking on this journey and that a child would be going along. This lady wanted to see me before leaving. In Cuba, many people are superstitious and very spiritual. This woman was a "Santera." A Santera is someone of the Santeria faith who is considered a high priestess and practicing healer. People in the Santeria faith believe individuals have a destiny with God, a destiny fulfilled with the aid and energy of the spirits of the "Orishas". It's a religion that places a strong emphasis on divination through supernatural or mystical means. Santeria is deeply ingrained in Cuban culture and has influenced various aspects of life, including music, art, and folklore. My Mom, however, didn't believe in any of that and was reluctant to go see her, but with pressure from those around us was convinced to take me to the woman. I figured that she felt like she didn't have anything to lose by taking me. I'm sure when you've put it all on the line in faith, you're desperate for any sign from God or a divine power that it'll all work out, especially when it involves your only child.

WET FEET

The lady's home wasn't too far from where we were, so Mom and I made our way to her by walking there. We didn't go alone though, a woman from the house we were staying in came with us. I believe she knew the Santera. When we got there, I remember thinking the outside of the house looked creepy and sort of unkept with very large trees surrounding the house and wild bushes overtaking and crowding the outside walls of the small home. The lady greeted us at the door before we got to the doorstep. She received my mom and the lady that was with us and then looked at me and said, "this is him, yes", with a big smile on her face. We made our way in, and the house was dark without much sunlight coming in from the outside, it didn't help that it was already late in the afternoon. The house had an overwhelming smell of incense and tobacco. The Santera asked my Mom if she could see me alone. My Mother agreed and waited in the living room as I slowly followed the lady into the back room of the house. This room had a shrine filled with weird artifacts and all sorts of things I had no clue about.

Although the room felt frightening, there was something about the lady that made me feel calm. She sat me down in front of her and grabbed my hands. She told me I was about to embark on a great adventure but a dangerous one, but that the journey would be successful and that no one would get hurt because they were carrying something with them- me. She said I would be the reason we would make it safely, but for us to make it out safely, I needed to carry something with me. She took out an 8 x 10 piece of white Styrofoam with a picture of the "La Virgen de la Caridad del Cobre" or Lady of Charity taped to the foam. The "Caridad del Cobre" is a popular Marian title for the Blessed Virgin Mary known in the Catholic religion. The Virgin is one of the island's most treasured religious figures, representing hope and salvation in the face of misfortune. She holds great significance in Cuban culture, spirituality, and history and is considered the patroness of the country. She also serves as a symbol of protection at sea, some say more so for kids. The Virgin holds a special place in the hearts of many Cubans, both on the island and in the diaspora. The lady told me to hold onto the foam with the paper picture of the saint during the trip, and by doing so, she said I would not be harmed as well as those going on the journey with me. I kept eye contact with her the entire time she was explaining all this to me, and although I didn't fully understand all that she was talking about, I knew it was serious. Before leaving she performed a small ritual on me that involved flowers, herbs, and lots of cigar smoke. I took her directions to heart, took the Styrofoam with the photo, and thanked her. I don't remember her name.

It was already nightfall when we returned to the house, and we met the rest of the group that was coming on the trip. There were eight of us: five men, two women, and me, the only child. The men consisted of the captain, and ironically his name was Jesus, his two sons who were in their 20s, Jesus and Ernesto, and two strangers my Mom and I had never met before, Frank and Pablo. Then there were the two women, my Mom and a lady from our home neighborhood, Maricel, whose daughter went to school with me, but Maricel, had decided to come on the voyage without her.

The vessel we were going on was an actual makeshift raft, entirely man-made. The raft consisted of eight black rubber inner tubes from truck tires that were tied together with rope, wood panels, and a thick fabric that they attached to the bottom to serve as protection for us from sea animals. Materials that reveal the resourcefulness of a Cuban balsero. There were no sides to lean against to rest our bodies; all we had were the tubes that we'd sat in and each other. I don't know exactly who put the raft together or how long it took to complete it; all I know is the raft was ready to go that day.

The raft looked something like this:

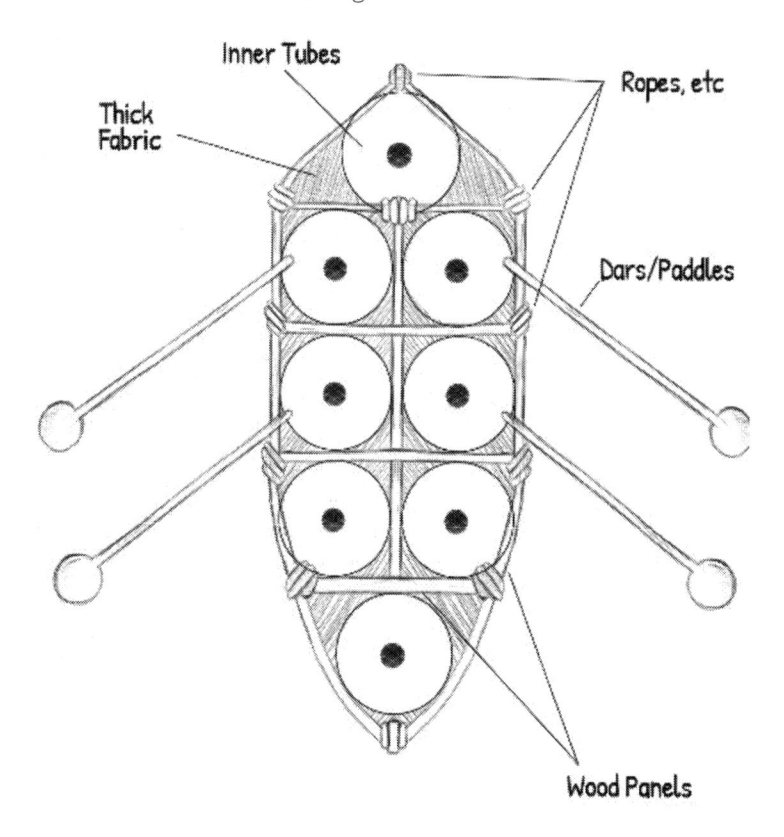

Inner Tubes
Thick Fabric
Ropes, etc
Oars/Paddles
Wood Panels

Because people in Cuba were attempting to escape by way of the sea, as it was practically the only way out, the government was on high alert, constantly detaining people. For that reason, we had to leave close to the middle of the night. Once it was a little past eleven o'clock at night, we began getting onto the raft. I was told to sit right in the middle of the raft, and my Mom was in the tube next to me. I could tell by her face that she was in some way in disbelief that she was about to finally realize her ultimate dream of leaving Cuba. I had the kid's floaty on me and a rope tied between the floaty and the raft as a precaution, just in case, at any point, the raft would flip over. Some of the grownups, including the captain, told my Mom I should take a sleeping pill to help me fall asleep. My Mom immediately refused and told them she wanted me to be alert at all times and not be under the influence of any medication. She was worried that being in a state of daze could be dangerous in a moment of panic. Besides, my Mother knew the type of kid I was. I was a smart boy and was always thinking quickly on my feet. And again, I was never afraid of the ocean, and she knew that. She knew it was best for me to be aware of my surroundings and of what was happening and be there for each other. One by one, we each got in the raft. The moment all eight of us were on it, the weight automatically pushed the raft down, almost to sea level, which meant that we would easily get wet from any slight movement from the raft. At first, it was a bit cold and incredibly uncomfortable especially since I was already tired and as a young boy, accustomed to being asleep in bed by this hour. We hadn't even left the garage yet. What is this, I thought to myself, clinging onto the foam picture that was given to me, but then I looked at my Mom, and she reassured me. Immediately, I felt calm. As long as she was alright, I was too. The captain instructed us before heading out to duck down and stay quiet. A piece of dark fabric was put over all of us to conceal us even more. No one was rowing at this point, but the raft began to move. At first, I didn't know how it was moving as no one in the raft was talking or moving but then I figured out there were two guys in scuba gear that were pushing us slowly out to sea, as far as they possibly could. It seemed like they moved us for quite some time. Once we were significantly out from the main coast, the two men in scuba gear said bye to the captain and headed back inland. As soon as we lifted the black cover from us, I was amazed at how bright the stars were. It felt like we were in a beautiful painting. The water was still, and the starlight glistened off the water perfectly. The men on the raft now began to row the wooden paddles moving us slowly further out to sea. I remember seeing the coastal line getting further away until I nodded off to sleep next to my Mom.

On the morning hours of May 1, 1991, I woke up in the middle of the ocean. The picture in my mind of that morning is still very vivid. The sun was only just rising slowly behind the horizon, and the ocean water was completely flat and eerily still while a multitude of colors decorated the ocean top as the morning light struck the sea. The rays glistened over the very placid ocean water. It looked like we were sailing on a pool of crystals, like diamonds twinkling and dancing across the water. The beauty of it literally took my breath away. The air was crisp, and although we all were part wet, the imagery of seeing our little raft slowly move further out felt dream-like, so calm and peaceful. Behind us, we could see Cuba, almost like a thin smoke in the far distance. Everything I had ever known, up until that point, I was now leaving behind with nothing more than a glimmer of hope and a life ahead that I couldn't identify or knew what it would bring. It was the last time I saw my country.

Something I didn't realize then, my Mom and I never knew how long this journey would take prior to heading out. It was never discussed. There was never a concrete timeline. This was a shot in the dark. None of us knew how long this trip would take via a raft but somehow it truly didn't matter because the urgent need to escape the repression was far more real. It outweighed any thought of things going wrong. I am sure, Jesus, the captain, had an idea of a potential timeframe but never the outcome it turned out in the end. We had a few days' worth of food that consisted mostly of canned goods such as spam, Russian canned beef; Soviet products that were a staple in Cuba at the time, a bag full of boiled eggs still in its shells, fruits (mostly oranges and tangerines), and a few gallons of water. We didn't realize on that first day that one of the gallons of water was contaminated with gasoline. I guess whoever filled it with water made the careless mistake of not cleaning the gallon before filling it with water. As a result, that shortened our already limited water supply even more.

Everyone began to wake up that first morning, and although everyone was in good spirits, some felt seasick, and it was only made worse by trying to eat the boiled eggs we packed. A few immediately hung their bodies over the raft and threw up, myself included. The mixture of throw- up and eggshells in the water attracted a shark to the surface, and its size was quite large. Out of the tranquil ocean a huge hammerhead appeared before us as its dorsal fin broke the surface of the water. We all sat still and quiet as the captain motioned to us not to talk. It circled us several times for what seemed like half an hour and eventually left, but the sudden realization of the threats we were facing out at sea left us feeling uneasy. It was the only time we saw a shark up close like that, but throughout the voyage, we were being bumped underneath by large fishes, most likely curious sharks. The fabric placed on the bottom of the raft was thick and never once gave way to the turbulent conditions of the ocean. Thank God.

The first day at sea was fun. Everyone was in great spirits and having a bit of premature celebration, singing random tunes, and making silly jokes about Fidel Castro. The sea was calm, and despite us having a short food and water supply, everything seemed the be going ok. Throughout the day, I'd randomly grab the foam picture of the saint and bring it closer to me; remembering the woman's words gave me comfort. The bottom of the picture included the image of people on boats looking up at her in prayer. I remember looking at it for hours studying every detail. During the middle of the day, the sun was beaming down at us ferociously with nowhere to hide from it. My Mom would cover me with the small blanket she brought with her. It was the only thing we had that provided some shade. As night approached, the clear sky was slowly getting covered with thunderclouds, a storm was clearly visible ahead of us. The waves began to pick up. At first, the waves only rocked the raft quickly back and forth, and then as they got bigger, they washed over our entire bodies. It felt like the time between each wave was getting smaller and smaller. The sea became something out of a horror film. There was zero visibility. It was so dark at times, and with the waves splashing over us for what felt like every second, I could barely see my Mom, who was right next to me. I could only feel her. The only time I could see my own hands was when lightning illuminated the sky for seconds at a time. The thunder clapped loudly, threatening us after each bolt of lightning that seemed like it was too close for comfort. I held on tight to the wood that was keeping our raft together. It often felt like my hands were bleeding because I was gripping them so hard. The waves whipped our raft in all directions. The most terrifying thing is to hear a wave coming towards us but not be able to see it coming. All of us would brace for each massive wave. Everyone decided to pile over each other, with the men on top and me under everyone as we braced the gigantic waves over and over throughout the night. It was a constant and relentless rhythm of rain and waves hitting us. Although we were in the Caribbean in May, we were freezing. None of us got any sleep, and many of us were sick to our stomachs from swallowing sea water and the movement of the raft.

Morning light began to appear, barely breaking through the dark clouds. The day started very somber with light rain. The sea looked different now compared to the way it looked the first morning. The ocean water was so much darker, almost black- she looked mad. Although I wasn't scared of the ocean before, its color out at sea did frighten me. The further we headed out to nowhere, the waves got larger. It felt like we were on a rollercoaster ride that had no ending in sight. It was a constant up and down movement. One moment we would be at the bottom of a wave with a massive wall of water of the next wave right next to us. I looked up in both awe and panic at the gigantic body of water coming toward us. It looked surreal.

I don't think the word exhaustion fully defines the feeling of being cold, wet, scared, tired, and sick to your stomach from being whipped back and forth relentlessly. We quickly found out that most of the food we had left was lost at sea from the storm during the night and we were left with one single gallon of water. Nothing could have prepared us for how brutal that first storm hit us. It came so fast we didn't have time to gather the supplies and cover them under us. Our immediate instinct was to grab onto anything we could to try to stay on and not be swept away off the raft. The entire second day was spent surviving multiple storms. The powerful sea became an adversary, its immense power reminding us of our own insignificance in the face of nature's forces. We got no breaks, and all of us had now been awake for well over 24 hours. Midday, the captain shouted that the compass was broken. We all looked at each other right before a huge wave hit. Nothing more was said. What could be said? An overwhelming feeling of uncertainty was felt as we were now without a true sense of direction. Mom hugged me tight in her arms. I remember her whisper to me that she loved me. She had a way of making me feel like everything was going to be okay and I believed it because she was there by my side. Nightfall was approaching, and the storm hadn't let up, not even for a second, and more storms appeared to follow. Once again, all of our bodies huddled together as waves and rain slammed against us. The only hope that I seemed to have was the picture in the foam that was surprisingly still intact. I clung to it as if my life depended on it because perhaps it did. There wasn't much sleep at night, only lots and lots of prayers.

CHAPTER 6

FEAR EXPOSED

For reasons that still aren't well understood, human skin starts to break down after continuous immersion in water after only a few days. You'd suffer open soars and be liable to fungal and bacterial infections just from the spores on your skin, even if the water itself was perfectly sterile. The Chinese government has been accused of immersing political prisoners up to the neck as a form of torture, and victims are reportedly unable to stand or use any of their major muscles for several weeks after immersion of just a few days.

- Divya Serigal, BBC Science Focus

FEAR EXPOSED

There are some experiences that are etched in our minds for the rest of our lives. Moments that stand still in our thoughts and appear like frames from a film. We carry it with us, and they become a part of who we are. Maybe it isn't so much just the experience that molds us, but the feelings we experience during these moments that make their mark, especially in the face of mortality. All I know is that the third day out at sea are moments that I will never forget. I can close my eyes and see everything like it were in front of me and feel the same feeling of terror that I had as a child out at sea. I can still remember my Mom's face when she saw me cry for the first time on this voyage.

Cold and wet, day three began with barely any sunlight as the day was full of clouds. Dark storm clouds loomed overhead, obscuring the sun and casting a gloomy shadow over the turbulent sea. The dark grey sky creepily enhanced the deep dark depth of the open ocean. It wasn't raining yet, but it didn't matter. The sea was so active that its massive waves constantly made sure we stayed wet. The wind howled, whipping up massive waves that crash against our frail vessel, threatening to capsize it at any moment. None of us had any sleep, still. It was impossible to be in any state of relaxation. The tumultuous environment demanded our attention. I became hyper-aware of the waves' magnitude, their crashing sounds, and the way they engulf the raft. My focus intensified as I closely observed the movements of the waves and the raft's response to them. It was exhausting. Each wave felt like it hit harder than the last, and there was always another one that seemed to follow.

Despite the men maneuvering the raft with the oars, we realized the limited control we had over the situation. We had no choice but to surrender to the power of the waves, accepting that we must trust the raft and its ability to weather the storm. It continued like that for the rest of the day. How our raft was still intact at that point is beyond me. I can't help but think that the picture of the Caridad del Cobre had something to do with it. It was still in the foam placeholder, and I hadn't let it go at all.

We had no idea which direction to row in or knew where we were headed without a working compass. Our food supply was practically all gone. The only food that hadn't been ravished by the storm or eaten were a few tangerines that my Mom and Maricel hung onto for dear life. Even worse, our water supply was down to only a gallon. The rest vanished during prior storms. Thankfully, we were able rely on rainwater and kept our one gallon full while we could. Weirdly no one said anything about the fact that our supply was now next to nothing even though we all knew it, sort of like an unspoken understanding. There was nothing any of us could do to change the situation, and we all knew what it meant to be lost at sea without enough food and drinking water. The sky began to turn dark orange as night approached, and there was a heavy dread amongst us because what came with the dark hours of the night was never good. None of us said a word- the silence spoke volumes between us. All of us wanted the same thing- to get off the raft, out of the water, even if it meant going back to Cuba and facing the wrath of our government. We didn't care. The only sound amongst us was that of the storm and the sound of the waves.

Nothing but the ocean was around us as far as the eye could see. The sheer vastness of ocean water was intimidating. More than ever before, I felt its raw power every second of being out there on the raft and it was very unsettling. We were under its mercy, and I never felt so small. The sea was turbulent and really menacing. I had never seen it that dark before. I was no longer in the crystal-clear waters of my beautiful home island of Cuba. When I looked down, I saw nothing but darkness, a bottomless pit ready to swallow us. Often with the waves continuously hitting us repeatedly, I couldn't see anyone from the group sitting right next to me. I remember feeling scared, like on the brink of screaming out loud but I didn't. Prior to us leaving on this voyage, I would sometimes hear adults in our neighborhood talk about other groups of Cubans leaving on rafts and never hearing from them again. Some would speculate that they met their end drowning. They would repeat to one another that the ocean was unforgiving. That word, unforgiving, stood out to me. I never understood why they were calling it unforgiving. The only side of the ocean I was familiar with was beautiful and somewhat calm. Never like this, never like it was now at this moment. I had now met the unforgiving ocean that was also treacherous as she is beautiful. I was now the one facing it and I didn't want to drown. I didn't want to die. It was hard for me as a child to shake that thought away, especially with the very real circumstances I found myself in. As time went by without any sign of rescue or land, feelings of desperation were setting in quickly. One of the most challenging aspects of being lost at sea is accepting the unknown. Uncertainty becomes constant. Not knowing if someone would find us or if help was near. This psychological strain was a lot for me to control, and as I grappled with the wariness of the situation, my emotions kept swinging between hope and despair.

Then on the distant horizon, we saw a speckle of a boat, and it appeared to be coming in our direction. It was our first time seeing a boat since we started our journey. We all screamed as we had never screamed before, waving our hands. The men were trying to stand up and wave. We continued like that for a while as the ship got closer and closer. As the distance between us and the boat got smaller, our hope of being rescued grew. The men started paddling our raft in its direction. We were so close to this nightmare being over, we could almost breathe a sigh of relief. That feeling was taken away as fast as it came when we noticed that nobody from the ship was coming outside to direct us, with no signs of movement or of anyone that spotted us. The ship wasn't slowing down, and there were huge waves and whirlpools being created because of its large size. Our raft kept getting stuck in the twisting surges of water made by the ship, and every time we tried to paddle closer, it caused the raft to shake back and forth violently. We were so close that if the boat had turned only a couple of feet in our direction, it would have gone over us. We screamed even louder, hoping someone would hear. They couldn't see us at this point, our tiny raft was much smaller than the ship, and we probably looked like nothing but a tiny dot out in the dark ocean under the almost nightfall and cloudy sky.

The back of the ship was about to pass us when the men stopped paddling in fear of getting close to the immense velocity the ship's propellers make in the water. The massive currents the vessel made in the back end were much stronger, and we did have a moment of panic where we thought the raft would tip over. We all held on tight to the rope, wood, and anything we could grab onto as the ship passed us completely. We stopped yelling. For a few seconds, we stood there, and we all looked at each other in silence. The enormous ship continued on as if nothing had happened. To this day, I have this haunting image in my head of quietly sitting there as I watched the boat get further away and the tiny ribbon of light left in the sky disappearing before us. It was in that instant that an unfamiliar feeling took over me: fear. I never felt true fear until that point in my life. Fear showed itself, and it was frightening and powerful. I couldn't transcend it or shake it, the situation I was in hit me all at once in that one moment, and I had this realization that this was how

FEAR EXPOSED

we were going to die. The group's silence was quickly broken by a child's cry as I began to weep uncontrollably. All the fear and tears I had been holding back were so overwhelming that I couldn't stop them. I could feel death hanging over us. I looked straight into my Mother's eyes, and for the first time on this journey begged her to take me back; all my Mom could do was cry back and hold me tight in her arms.

A sense of hopelessness consumed every being in that raft, and the rest began to cry, also. I finally realized the full scope of danger of our situation, just how dire it really was, and my heart sank. I saw the grown men cry out and sob like children. I was sobbing and continued pleading with my Mom to take me back to Cuba. I cried out to see my cousins and aunts. She could do nothing but look at me with extreme guilt and regret and fear as she herself sobbed. The situation engulfed me with hopelessness, my mind was racing with memories of loved ones and the life I once had. Regret and sorrow mingled with my fading strength, as I faced the grim possibility of not making it out alive. My Mom reached for me, and we hung onto each other, knowing that we were going to die at sea with each other. As I write this, no matter how hard I try, there are no words to fully describe the feeling of knowing you are going to watch your Mother die and your Mother knowing that she is going to watch her son die. We wanted to get off the raft, out of the water, and run, run far away, but we couldn't. We were stuck, forced to face death that seemed not too far away.

Our tears were met with rain as the night brought us more storms. It now became a routine of sorts as I lay back against my Mother, and we all piled against each other as we drifted in submission to the wind and waves without a sense of direction. I looked down at my saint with tears in my eyes and, in my head, spoke to her with so much urgency. I called out to her for protection and for a miracle. Most of all for us to get rescued and be out of this deadly monstrous ocean. And with that, I gained a little bit of hope again. Although still bleak, it helped me to endure another cold, wet night.

CHAPTER 7

PUNISHED BY THE ELEMENTS

Human kidneys can only produce urine that's slightly less salty than salt water. So, in order to remove the extreme amount of sodium taken in by salt water, we urinate more water than we actually drank, and dehydration sets in. The body tries to compensate for the fluid loss by increasing the heart rate and constricting blood vessels to maintain blood pressure and flow to vital organs. You're also most likely to feel nausea, weakness, and even delirium. As you become more dehydrated, the coping mechanism fails. If you still don't drink any water to reverse the effects of excess sodium, the brain, and other organs receive less blood, leading to coma, organ failure, and eventually death.

- Vicki M. Giuggio, How Stuff Works

PUNISHED BY THE ELEMENTS

Deep into the night, the waves began to pick up, each time growing in size and slamming into us over and over again. Every time I opened my mouth to gasp for air, I was hit in the face by another wave, forcing me to gulp down sea water while trying to breathe. We all were. We couldn't see the moonlight. It was darker than anything you can imagine, and the only time we could see each other or even the waves was when we heard the thunder, and the lightning would strike in the distance throughout the night. One of the waves crashed into us so hard that it almost toppled the raft over, and I was knocked out of my tube in the raft, but my Mom's instant reflex saved me by literally grabbing me by the hair and pulling me towards her. It was continuous instances like that that made us fear and dread the nighttime. As every minute and hour went on, it was taking a toll on me, and I was feeling physical and mental exhaustion. I remember feeling cold, and hungry. My body was aching from sitting and laying down for what was now over 72 hours. No matter how much I wanted to find a bit of comfort there simply wasn't any. I was very thin, and I could feel the strain and irritation of having the bones of my body against the wood on the raft for so long. Especially during those hours of being stuck in a single position for so long as we held on tight managing to ride out the storms. I was experiencing fatigue and muscle cramps. I couldn't feel much of my legs either. I was numb from my waist down. Being wet makes everything ten times worse, I wanted to feel dry so bad.

Break of day came and gave us just that. The sun finally appeared fully out and visible, and the ocean was calmer. We discovered that we lost half of our oars, leaving us with just two. You'd think the sun rising would be a relief, but it wasn't. In fact, it was the exact opposite, with the hot sun beaming down on us. In the early hours of the morning, it was nice at first but by noon we could feel the sweltering heat. I lost my blanket and had nothing to cover me from the sun. We could feel our skin slowly cooking under the rays of the sun, and there was nowhere to run to or hide under. There was nothing we could do but sit in it and feel the pain. Time felt like it was passing in slow motion; every minute felt like hours.

There was a huge shift in energy on this day that was unmistakable. The group barely spoke to one another. Not only were we drifting away at sea, but our minds were also. There was nothing to do and the sun made us sleepy. Some of us, like me, would be asleep for most of the day given that the sea became calmer, or at least we tried to, even though part of our bodies was aching and burning. Others were constantly scanning the horizon, praying for the sight of a passing ship or the sound of a distant airplane. But the vast emptiness mocked our longing for salvation. Time becomes an enigma as we drifted aimlessly, unsure if anyone will ever come to our rescue. The days blurred together, as hunger gnawed at my stomach and thirst parched my throat. We were so hungry and all we had were a few tangerines that we meticulously shared. We were surviving entirely on captured rainwater that was about run empty. We were facing threats from starvation and dehydration. It was becoming more difficult to get a grasp on reality. When people are sleep deprived, dehydrated, and under the sun for long periods of time, they start doing strange things because they begin to slowly lose their minds. Like a carpet being pulled underneath your feet, it happens suddenly, with no warning. Confusion sets in so fast that it makes it all that more real. Things were quickly becoming more desperate. Between the lack of fresh water and the cruel heat, I started to experience very vivid hallucinations. I started hearing voices and seeing things that weren't there. I listened to the familiar voices of my aunts and cousins that we left behind in Cuba calling out to me. I would hear them call out my name over and over. I would see people in the water, grouped together in the distance staring at me. Some had familiar faces, others had their faces blurred out. It felt like I was in a dream, but I was very much awake. I started seeing tall buildings a few yards from us, towering high above the water, and palm trees all around us. I saw something that looked like a marina, with many boats everywhere. I saw a long white fence that was paralleled to our raft right beside us, and it all looked so real. Perhaps they were things I wanted to see, some sort of lifeline. I made attempts to say something out loud, to alert the others in the raft, but my throat was super dry and prevented me from screaming. Some images would appear and stay visible long enough for me to see details like the sun reflecting off the window glass of buildings appearing in front of me. Other images came and went swiftly. I rubbed my eyes several times, closing them tight and reopening them slowly. When they all were still there, I felt confused about why we were still in the raft suffering. I shook my Mom so that she could see it too. I pointed them out to her and asked her, "There's a building there? Why can't we just walk there?" She looked at me with her eyes filled with so much sadness and pulled me closer to her and held me and whispered to me that there was nothing there as tears fell from her eyes.

I experienced so many quiet moments, where I would completely zone out and have intimate moments just staring out into the ocean, specifically at the horizon. The horizon is such a peculiar thing. After days of being in the ocean, the horizon line felt like something tangible just an arm's length away. But the absence of visual cues can contribute to the deceiving nature of the horizon. It's just a single constant line where the sky meets the Earth's surface when viewed from a specific vantage point. My visual perception saw it as a long endless wall. And I thought that behind it, I would find the United States. I thought I could reach it, that I was getting near it, but I never did of course. It plays tricks in your mind, almost like the goal was to get to that horizon, except you would never reach that goal because it just doesn't exist. As frustrating as it was, ironically, it still served a purpose in my mind. It became my motivation; the goal was to reach the horizon line as if that were our destination, no matter how far off I would always be from it. Metaphorically, the horizon can represent possibilities and dreams. That's what it did for me, it gave me so much hope. In a strange way, it kept my mind going, constantly inviting me to contemplate the mysteries of the world and the limitless potential that can lie ahead.

In a moment of hope, a small light brown colored bird landed on our raft. I knew this time I wasn't hallucinating because everyone reacted to it. The bird landed in front of our raft, and the adults immediately thought that it meant that there was land nearby, and we all started looking around anxiously, expecting to see land but we never saw any. The bird rested on the raft for a few minutes and eventually left.

Every once in a while, we would feel fishes, most likely sharks, slamming our raft from underneath. We couldn't see what it was since we had that thick fabric protecting us from total exposure to the water beneath, but that didn't change the fact that we could still feel it. It was very creepy and unnerving. We saw a pod of dolphins go by, and I tried savoring each second of watching them because they have always been one of my favorite sea animals. It was one of the few moments where I found myself smiling. I tried to find delight in the small things around us because if I didn't, my mind would venture off to focus on how hungry and thirsty I was and how much my body ached. There were huge colorful iridescence-like fishes that circled our raft during the day. In the nighttime, sometimes the water around us would illuminate with little blue, bright dots everywhere. There were hundreds of tiny fishes moving all around our legs. By this time, the innertubes were showing signs of having lower air pressure. The raft was now completely submerged in the water, which meant that from our waist down we were all wet, due to our weight and the condition our raft was in.

Sometimes during the night, we'd see red lights far away in the distance. I'd nod off in half awaken sleep state, listening to the adults quietly discuss them and how they thought that the lights were from nearby ships. Dozing off to sleep and listening to them talk about this gave me hope, something to hang onto with the picture that my arms were still wrapped around. Hope is what I believe kept me alive. Hope that we'd still be rescued soon. I knew that it had to be soon. I could feel it. We didn't have much time left.

By the fifth day, small sores started showing on our legs, like something was eating our skin. We weren't sure if it was a combination of our skin starting to break off after being immersed in the salt water for so long or if it was the small fishes around us biting the sensitive skin, but we all had it, and it only added to the painful discomfort we were already in. Already dehydrated and dying of thirst, we all had this extreme urge to drink salt water. With so much body of water around us, it was so tempting to consider drinking it as a desperate measure. Ernesto, the captain's son, couldn't resist temptation and drank some of the salt water, which prompted him to vomit instantly. The stunt, driven by his clouded mind, left him feeling weaker.

By this day, no one was talking to one another. The silence was incredibly poignant and evocative. It indicated a deep sense of shared understanding, of tension, contemplation, and sadness among all of us. With that also came moments of conflict. One of the guys in the group was named Frank. I'll never forget his name because it's my dad's name. He was seated at the very front of the raft and never spoke to any of us from the very first day. He never even turned around to engage in conversation. Out of nowhere, Maricel, the other lady in the group, began picking on him and would scream at him. She would shout, "We have to kill him!" over and over. She was convinced the reason we hadn't reached land or gotten rescued was because of him. The delirium from dehydration, the heat, and hunger was setting in. Mind you, we were all technically on top of each other with barely any space between us, so someone shouting sounded extremely loud, and to all of us, it put our nerves on edge. She was being aggressive with her words and rambling incoherently. He could clearly hear her, but still, he wouldn't react to it. He never turned around or said anything back. My Mom and the captain,

Jesus, tried their best to talk to her in hopes of calming her down, but nothing worked. It was very unnerving and had us all worried. The captain had a huge knife that he brought on the raft with him in case of an emergency. After Maricel started her tangent, he threw the knife out into the ocean because he was worried that she would get a hold of it and stab Frank during the night. He knew that he was too weak to fight her off, so he ultimately made the decision to throw our only protection out into the ocean.

My Mom was terrified because she knew that if a fight broke out, chances are the raft would flip or I would get hurt in the process. I remember hearing my Mom tell the captain that if something was to happen to her for whatever reason, to not let anyone hurt me. She begged him. I stared at her wanting to cry and I wanted to tell her to stop, but I was too weak to move. The situation was becoming more distressing. Hope was fleeting rapidly, and anguish was overtaking everyone onboard. I kept holding tight to my saint in the foam, still intact all those days later.

The fifth night was, for the most part, calm. A half-moon could be seen so clearly, with an expanse of millions of stars seemingly illuminating endlessly across the night sky. I dozed off sometime at night but was awakened by an argument between the captain and Pablo. He was screaming and crying and shouting at the captain to take him back. Apparently, he threw the last two oars we had into the water. His anxiety drove him to throw the oars into the water out of desperation. The captain was calmly trying to tell him the compass was still broken and that he didn't know where "back" was. He didn't even know where we were. We all watched the last of the oars float away. We let them. We figured out what is the point anyway. As the raft drifted to nowhere, I could hear my mom whispering a plea to God under her breath. It was my first time ever hearing her pray.

By morning we were completely zoned out. Day 6 was weighing heavily on me. The taste of saltwater lingered on my chapped lips, a constant reminder of our desperate surroundings. Exhaustion and dehydration consume my body, weakening my muscles and clouding my thoughts. The eerie silence among us was loud in the midst of our quandary situation. I felt so weak. We were already a few days in without food or water. The physical and psychological challenges we were all facing by being adrift in the ocean were pushing the limits of our endurance. The sun was beating down hard on us without any protection from clouds. All of us had painful skin irritation from the constant exposure of salt water and the sun. The sky was clear blue, and the sea was much calmer compared to the other days. Even though we were all close in proximity to one another, I felt the distance between me and everyone else on the raft. The vastness of the open sea made me feel incredibly isolated. Without any land in sight, I began to experience a profound sense of loneliness. My mind was just wandering away. Almost as if I was floating on air, like an out-of-body experience. I began to lose my ability to distinguish my surrounding, of those around me, including my Mother. Their faces seemed blurred as if my eyes were covered in salt water. I felt my soul drifting away from me. My whole being light as a feather, my insides hollow and empty. I hadn't eaten properly in days yet I wasn't hungry anymore. I was passed beyond hunger at this point. I was no longer feeling like myself. Strangely, I wasn't scared, I just felt peace. My face was burned from the sun. My lips were severely cracked and full of pus. My legs were beyond numb and with gash-like holes on my exposed skin.

As we sat there in silence, someone yelled out, "SHIP!!!".

CHAPTER 8

CLIMAX OF THE LOST ONES

"Hope itself is like a star—not to be seen in the sunshine of prosperity, and only to be discovered in the night of adversity."

- Charles Haddon Spurgeon

CLIMAX OF THE LOST ONES

Not knowing what is real or not is one of the scariest feelings, especially when you're a child, not fully understanding what's happening to your mind but knowing it's something bad. Awakening my dazed state by the shouting around me, I looked up and my eyes caught a glimpse of a distant shape on the vast stretch of water. It took a moment for my mind to comprehend what I was seeing. My eyes looked, but my brain took a few seconds to recognize that a large size ship, only a few yards from us, was heading right for us. I couldn't distinguish whether the ship was real or not. Was I imagining things again? It's a surreal moment that was challenging my perception of reality. When everyone on the raft started screaming out of joy, I knew then that it was, in fact, real. We were all so out of it that we didn't see the ship in the far distance until it was much closer. It must have been visible for quite some time though, as the day was perfectly clear. The sight of the ship ignited a spark of hope within all of us, hope that had significantly dwindled in the last couple of days. When the ship got closer, it blared its horn- another reminder that this was really happening. Suddenly, the possibility of rescue became real, and a surge of optimism rushed through my veins. We all tried to scream, as loud as our dry throats would allow us to. It was as if each of us had been invigorated with a renewed life force. The ship represented a lifeline, a chance for survival that we had almost given up on. It filled us with newfound strength. Eyes that had no tears to cry could cry now. Our voices that were faint and almost gone had come back. Our weak bodies gained the strength to act quickly, and when the boat got closer, the men lifted my feeble, weak body the highest they could get me so that the crew on deck could see there was a child on the raft. As they lifted me, I couldn't feel my legs at all, yet I felt the strongest I had in days. Real hope once again existed and even though none of us knew what was going to happen to us next or what consequences we were going to face for escaping, what we did know is that we were going to live to see another day that wouldn't be at sea.

The ship's horn continued to blow, and the closer it got we could see people running on the ship's decks and pointing at us. A wave of joy and elation flooded our entire beings. The despair and desolation that had consumed us for days was momentarily replaced by pure happiness. It was an emotional high, a sense of triumph over the extreme adversities we faced. Even though we had already seen people on the ship signaling to us, it still didn't stop us from continuing to shout, wave our arms, and from grabbing the attention of those on the ship, already expressing our gratitude and excitement. The ship slowed down and once it stopped completely near us, a man on a bullhorn speaker on deck began to communicate with us, but all I could understand was "Miami," and something about calling Miami. After a few minutes they said something like, "Miami said yes," which meant we could be rescued and taken there. Once again, we all rejoiced, hugged one another, and cried tears that felt endless.

This ship was a huge cargo ship traveling from Colombia to Miami. It was passing through the Gulf of Mexico when they spotted us. We were so far from both Cuba and the United States, heading deeper into the very rough waters of the Gulf of Mexico. If this ship didn't see us this day, we most likely would've died of dehydration and starvation or given into the elements out at sea. After six days at sea, it was just inevitable. The ship was a blessing sent by God, and there isn't a day that goes by that I don't thank God for it being sent our way.

The men on our raft began using their arms and hands to steer the raft closer to the ship. As we got near the ship, the waves would hit the ship and throw us back out again. The crew on the ship released a rope ladder down the side of the ship. The oldest son of the captain began to feel a lot of anxiety and became anxious wanting to jump to the water and swim towards the ladder. But the ocean was rough.

He suffered from epilepsy, so his father did his best to calm him down, he would hold him and would try to talk him out of it, preventing him from jumping and more so prevent him from an epileptic episode which could be dangerous not only for him but everyone on board the raft. It was a scary moment. Finally, a man from the ship went down the ladder, using a long stick with a hook, when the raft got close enough, he was able to grab on and tie the raft to the ladder.

As if all these events that had unfolded so fast weren't unbelievable enough, I looked down at the picture of the saint I was holding during the journey, and it began to crumble before my eyes. After six days at sea and constantly being wet, miraculously the paper stayed intact until that very moment we were being rescued. I looked at my mom in astonishment and with just a glance at each other we knew it meant something beyond our understanding. I let the foam, with pieces of the photo still intact, go for the first time since we left Cuba. I truly believe the saint had a part in our rescue, and that there were forces influenced by a divine or transcendent power, beyond my understanding, that got us to cross paths with the ship. I was thankful- we were thankful.

The first person to be led up the ladder was the captain's son, to prevent him from having a potential seizure. Then it was my turn. Because I was a child, weak and dehydrated, I didn't have the strength to move at all. A guy from the ship came down the ladder, grabbed me and put me on his back. I gathered the little strength that I had left and put my arms around his neck and tried to hold on as he carried me up the ladder. The ship was quite large, and it was a good distance to reach the top. I remember feeling my hands starting to slip, I had nothing left in me, but I heard my Mom's voice from below me shouting out to hold on. It gave me the strength I needed to make it to the top. I will never forget the feeling when they put me down on the ground, to feel something solid and dry again. The hard sturdy deck floor awakened the soles of my feet and the sensation continued up my legs. It made them feel alive again even though I didn't have the strength to stand. I sat on the deck shivering cold and the crew gave me a blanket to cover me while I waited with a lot of anxiety for my Mom to be onboard. She was one of the last ones to come up and every minute was excruciating for me. She was finally being helped onboard and as her body was being lifted over the top deck, my Mom's sunburned thighs scrapped the railing. She let out a scream in agony. Although she was in pain, I could see she was happy she had made it up. They laid her down next to me and immediately we hugged each other tight and cried out loud. Miraculously, all eight of us survived. A sense of shock and exhaustion was felt but somehow, I was feeling more alive than ever. The eight of us were all sitting on the floor crying as we all looked at each other knowing that we were on the brink of death, of watching each other slowly die. The captain of the ship and crew members stood around us in disbelief as well, not even knowing how long we had been out at sea, but I'm sure by the looks of us and the raft they could see that it was long enough. There are no words to describe the feeling of surviving such an ordeal. An overwhelming sense of relief consumed us, and I remember developing a deep appreciation for life just sitting there on that deck. So many emotions were washing over me. The whole moment felt very surreal. The ocean and this transcendent experience will forever be part of who I am.

I remember Jesus, our raft captain, was checking his pockets where he uncovered a few Cuban coins. He looked at every single one of us, without saying a word, just crying with happiness and suddenly threw the coins overboard. I felt that was his way of signifying closure and maybe a sense of relief for himself to know we made it out alive. It never occurred to me the immense pressure he must have felt to have the responsibilities that people's lives and wellbeing, including his two sons, were in his hands in a way. A crew member brought me the largest cup of milk I had ever seen. I had already loved milk, but that particular cup of milk after not having eaten or drank anything in days was the best cup of milk that I'd ever tasted in my life. Someone from the ship was videotaping us the whole time. They even captured us being rescued- the whole thing. I remember they showed us a little bit of the rescue when we were getting situated on deck. It was so weird seeing it from another perspective. What I would do to see that footage now. I'm not sure what happened to the raft, but I do know the ship's crew picked it out of the water and put it on to the ship. I have no idea what they did to it afterwards. I know around that time of the 90's, because so many Cubans were fleeing the island by raft, some of the rafts that could be salvaged, were being put in a museum, at the time, in Key West, FL. I'd like to imagine that our raft is on display in some museum.

Back on the ship, they gave us food. Someone on board gave us medical attention and looked at the open sores I had on my legs. I was malnourished and weighed just shy of 28 pounds. Afterwards, they took us to our rooms, where we were going to stay for the night, as we would get to Miami the next morning. They also gave us clothing. I had trouble moving and walking around the ship, my legs were trying to remember how to walk again. One of the first things we did was to shower. I can't tell you how satisfying it felt the feeling of immersing myself in fresh water after days of saltwater exposure. It was incredibly refreshing. It might sound a bit silly, but it truly felt like a moment of purity that in a strange way helped me shed the physical reminders of my ordeal at sea. As if the fresh water signified a turning point in my journey, representing a transition from survival mode to a phase of recovery and renewal. Like a tangible reminder that I had emerged from a challenging situation and was now on the path to recovery, both physically and emotionally.

CLIMAX OF THE LOST ONES

Mom and I had the opportunity to go out on the deck and see the sunset. The ocean seemed so different post rescue. We marveled at its grandeur and beauty again but with a new sense of respect for its power and unpredictability. Even though we were now safe on a large ship, we still felt uneasy being out in the open ocean. We sat on the floor of the deck, just us two, looking out into the boundless body of water, and took a moment to reflect on the journey we had undertaken and the hope that brought us to this point. Feeling extremely lucky with such a great sense of gratitude for being alive.

Once we got situated, I remember feeling the heat coming out of my body. Parts of my body was severely burnt, everywhere I sat felt uncomfortable, and I couldn't sleep. As my mom and some of the others slept, I made my way into a room near our cabin that looked like a breakroom, and the small tv in the corner caught my attention. Some of the crew members were there. Without me asking, they changed the channel and put on a cartoon called, He- Man and the Masters of the Universe on for me. A couple of the crew members asked me a few questions in Spanish about the journey. Every single one of the crew members we met were so nice, including the captain, who I believe was American. He didn't speak Spanish, but he did take the time to have crew members translate for him anytime he spoke to us to be sure we understood what he said. They were all amazed with the whole ordeal and how we risked everything for freedom. I'm sure none of them could imagine their child going through such an experience. They just couldn't believe it, and neither could we.

They announced dinner and our group began to wake up and make their way to the breakroom I was in. Suddenly, we heard someone screaming and I could recognize the voice. It was my mom. She was crying and screaming, saying she couldn't see. They immediately rushed to her aide and brought her into the breakroom. I sat by her side and held her hand while the others tried to calm her down. I was super worried and confused. They told her that most likely she couldn't see due to her body reacting to the heat and sunburn. They gave her Tylenol and within the hour, she began to gain her sight back. We then ate our dinner, everyone around, some members of our group shared some of the harrowing moments with the ship captain and the crew. We also laughed a lot, enjoying each other's company.

CLIMAX OF THE LOST ONES

The ship's captain told us we would arrive in Miami by 6 am the following day. One by one we retired to our room cabins, but I couldn't get comfortable in my room due to my skin burn. My skin was aching, and the small cabin felt like an oven. My mom couldn't sleep either, so we decided to go to a room that was like a living room area that had a large u-shape couch and big windows all around. The room felt cold, which made it easier to combat the heat coming out of my body. Mom and I talked for like an hour about so many things. Mostly it was me asking her questions about what's to come. My anticipation about arriving to the U.S. was palpable, maybe that was also playing a part in me not being able to rest. There was a cloud hanging over us with a lot of anxiety and nervousness due to an expected significant change that was looming. I had so much curiosity about what would be awaiting us in the United States, regardless of all the uncertainties. I kept imagining the sights, sounds, and experiences that lied ahead, all of it consuming me with such a sense of wonder and anticipation of a new adventure. An adventure that was soon about to begin. The whole day felt very surreal and long. As I laid on that couch, I felt so safe, with so many thoughts running through my head. We never went back to our room and instead ended up falling asleep on the couch. I closed my eyes and slipped away into the best sleep I had in days.

An approximation of the location we were rescued from:

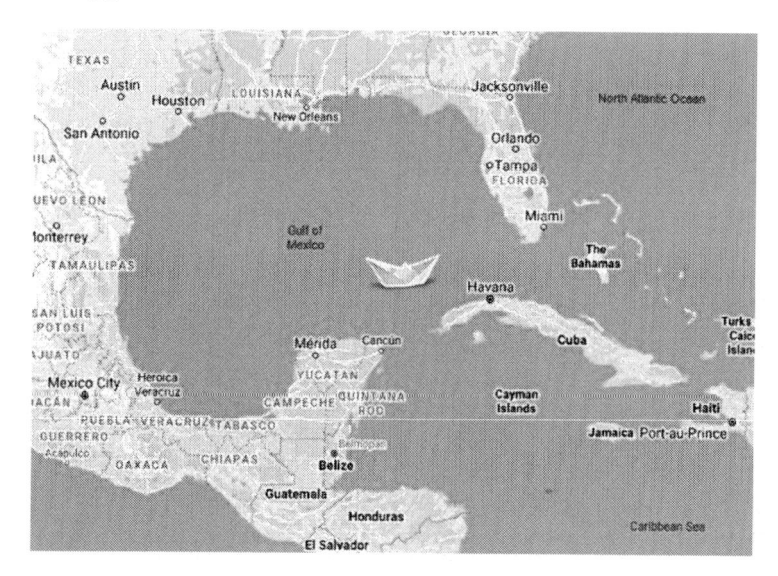

CHAPTER 9

WORLD OF LIGHTS AND FLYING CARS

"The power of imagination created the illusion that my vision went much farther than the naked eye could actually see."

- Nelson Mandela

WORLD OF LIGHTS AND FLYING CARS

Growing up in a third-world country as a young boy, America symbolized an unreachable star. A beacon of hope for those seeking a better future, a better life. In so many ways, the ultimate place to be but almost impossible for someone like me to ever achieve. I would hear whispers and snippets from people that would go visit the U.S. of an advanced society far more developed than anything I had ever seen in Cuba. I didn't see actual proof of it, so all I had was my imagination and a few points of reference from American films and music videos that were occasionally shown on a neighbor's small television. In my mind, America was something out of a sci-fi film, with a futuristic civilization where its cities lit up brightly, and cars flew. Mind you, that flying part bit was mostly due to me seeing Michael Jackson's Smooth Criminal video. I was fascinated. There were rumors that he owned flying cars, and all the kids in town ate it up, including me. For a kid like me, a simple object or a passing comment would help spark a cascade of imaginative thoughts and ideas. The world in Cuba very easily led me to construct narratives that transported me into fantastical imaginary worlds, because my real one was anything but. My imagination allowed me to blur the boundaries between the tough reality I was living and make-believe. That's one thing no one can take from you, because our imagination is not bound by the constraints of reality. And I dreamt, I dreamt big.

The ship's horns blew loudly, interrupting my deep sleep. We had just entered the Port of Miami. Mom and I were startled by a message on the speakers from the ship's captain. I quickly sat up in excitement, even though I was still half asleep. As we entered the port, I looked out the glass window. It was still dark out. The city of Miami was illuminated in all sorts of colored lights, with dozens of cars zooming by on the MacArthur Causeway. That is what was happening in real time; however, my eight-year-old eyes were registering something completely different. Suddenly, it dawned on me, and all I could interpret was that I was in the futuristic world I always fantasized about. In that moment, there were dazzling flashing lights and flying cars everywhere. I was witnessing the utopia world I always dreamt about when I imagined life in the U.S., a world that felt so foreign and unreachable at one point. It was now possible- I was there. I just stood by the window in awe as my mind was blown away by all that I saw before my very eyes. Just completely allowing the city's vibrancy and allure to captivate me in every way possible. The entire experience of approaching the port felt so thrilling and one that I will never forget. It was like a child walking up to Disney World for the first time, not knowing what to expect but knowing it was going to be amazing.

As I slowly came back to reality, the sun began to rise. The ship glided through the water, making its way to its port dock location. The water's shimmering surface and the tranquil beauty of the bay created an unforgettable visual experience. As we got closer to shore, I caught sight of the prominent Freedom Tower, standing tall like a gateway to the land of the free. A building that almost thirty years prior played a crucial role in the resettlement of thousands of Cuban refugees and ultimately became a symbol of hope and freedom for the Cuban community in Miami. Of course, I didn't know about the building's influential history that day we arrived, but it is not lost on me that it was one of the first things I saw on our first day in the United States.

All movement onboard stopped; the ship had now docked. Seven days after leaving Cuba, we officially made it to land. It felt so surreal. We all lined up by the exit. I was limping a lot as my legs and back were still in pain from the nightmare in the raft but I remember still feeling overwhelmed with so much excitement, anxiously awaiting the moment we had dreamed of as we began to disembark. Relieved, nervous, and thrilled, maybe we were a bit of all those emotions, but one thing we all truly felt was deep gratitude for being alive to see the shore of the United States. We said our goodbyes to the crew and thanked them again for what they did for us. Every single one of them was so incredibly kind, generous, and friendly. They were our saving grace in our moment of hopelessness. Without them, I wouldn't be here today.

The Coast Guards were waiting at the port for us, and as soon as we all got off the ship, they put us on a small boat that took us to another location on the opposite side of the port where the Miami police were waiting for us. I remember seeing the police in the distance as we were getting closer, and thinking it was cool seeing cops, not fully realizing we were in trouble. Immediately upon arrival, we were gathered outside the entrance of a single-story office building at the port where we were questioned by the police. The adults did all the talking, mostly Jesus, the captain, but the police did question everyone, including me. They asked me things like where I was from, how old I was, etc. Outside of the small office, there was a long table with donuts and coffee. I've never seen or had a donut before, and I kept eyeing the donuts thinking to myself, "What is that?" One of the cops saw me looking at it and let me have one. It was pure bliss. I sat there eating the donut watching the adults speak to the cops, and at that moment, there was nothing worrisome or wrong in my world.

The cops that spoke Spanish, told some of the people in our group that we were lucky to have made it to the U.S. alive. They informed us that just a few weeks before our arrival, a much larger group that also left Cuba in route to the U.S. weren't as lucky as half of them didn't make it and drowned during their voyage. There were so many groups coming ashore during that time period, that the Coast Guards kept a list of the Cubans arriving almost weekly. Mom and Maricel asked one cop if he could read some of the names as they were curious about one particular friend they knew from our hometown, who had left prior to us, and no one had heard from him in weeks. As the cop read them a list of survivors, they were happy to hear some familiar names but their friend from back home was not on the list. Shockingly, his name did appear on a list they had of Cubans who had perished at sea, witnessed by their fellow group members that did make it. I remember seeing my Mom and Maricel feeling sick to their stomachs to find out their good friend had died on his voyage. It was sad to know so many people weren't as lucky as we were. If it had not already, this tragic news would put it all that much more into perspective. None of us knew what was going to happen next, but we knew one thing; that no matter what, we were much better off than where we were lost at sea. The list of people perished was a reminder of that for us, and it made the unknown ahead a little more comforting for each of us.

Once inside the office, we did a lot of waiting around and underwent a series of further questioning from officials; a lot of it needing to be translated for us to understand it. Concurrently, immigration procedure papers were filed. This period during the early 1990's, a period known as the "Cuban rafters crisis" or "Balsero crisis," prompted specific immigration procedures for Cubans arriving in this manner. Not only were we lucky to have been rescued at sea, but we were also lucky to have done this journey in the time that we did. You see, prior to 1995, there was a law in place called the "Cuban Adjustment Act (CAA) of 1966," which allowed Cuban nationals who reached U.S. soil to apply for legal permanent residency after being physically present in the country for one year. This law applied to Cuban rafters as well, but most importantly, to Cuban rafters that didn't necessarily make it to U.S. soil themselves but that were intersected or rescued at seas, like me. So, because we came in 1991, we were automatically allowed to stay in the U.S. and given the privileged to pursue residency just a year later. By 1995, the Clinton Administration introduced the "Wet Foot, Dry Foot" policy which superseded the Cuban Adjustment Act. Under this new policy, if a Cuban national managed to reach U.S. soil ("dry foot"), they were generally allowed to stay and pursue legal residency. However, if intercepted at sea ("wet foot") by the U.S. Coast Guard or other authorities, they would typically be repatriated to Cuba.

The idea that everything happens for a reason at the right time is a belief often associated with the concept of fate or destiny. It suggests that events in our lives are not random or haphazard but are guided by a higher power or a predetermined plan. Many find solace in the idea that life's challenges and opportunities are part of a grander design or purpose. While it would be silly of me to say fate or destiny had nothing to do with me making it to the U.S., especially after everything I witnessed myself out there in the open ocean, I also ascribe to the idea that life is a product of a combination of chance, human choices, and external circumstances. All of it interconnected.

Inside the seaport office, I sat in a small chair quietly, hoping to pass the time with ease. A cop saw me there and came over to me and asked if he could take a picture of me with his polaroid camera. My Mom walked over and said to him it was fine. He took the picture and gave it to me to keep. A beautiful gesture on his part and one I've cherished ever since. To this day, I still have that photo. It is all I have of my journey, other than my memories. A reminder of my first day in the United States. They say a picture is worth a thousand words. The photo symbolizes so many things for me, but mostly it represents a journey of transformation, of an event that truly changed the course of my life forever. Of new beginnings and an understanding of the sacrifices my Mom made for us to get to where we are. The picture grounds me in my truth when I feel overwhelmed and reminds me that it could be much worse, that there are so many people that wish they could have the problems that I have today, that I am not only still breathing and alive, but I am now free. Looking at my photograph today evokes emotions in me that take me back to that eight-year-old boy, that from the moment he entered the Port of Miami, was already dreaming bigger.

WORLD OF LIGHTS AND FLYING CARS

The Polaroid Photo

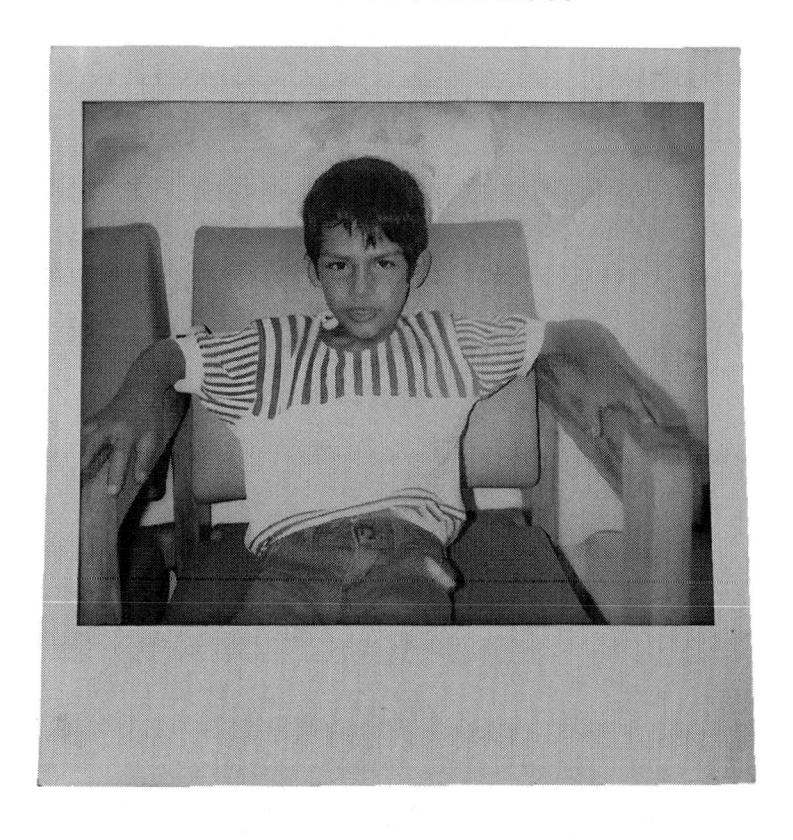

CHAPTER 10

LEARNING TO WALK...AGAIN

"Starting over is an acceptance of a past we can't change, an unrelenting conviction that the future can be different, and the stubborn wisdom to use the past to make the future what the past was not."

- Craig D. Lounsbrough

LEARNING TO WALK...AGAIN

The transition into any new beginning is always uncomfortable and a bit scary. I think being in any unknown territory can make us anxious, especially when you aren't sure where you will be tomorrow or where you'll live, or how you will survive. The level of faith a person must have to knowingly put themselves in this situation is unfathomable at times to me. It requires completely trusting God and the process to work it all out for you. This was exactly the place that we found ourselves in as we were led by the police into a van from the Port of Miami after spending hours waiting for our paperwork to be completed. I limped my way to the van excited to see more of this new world. I had no idea what a detention center was; some referred to it as a prison. We didn't know what to expect or what it would be like, but again, we trusted the process.

As we headed to the detention center of Krome located far west in Miami, Florida, I spent the long ride looking out the window in wonder. Miami's tropical climate was very reminiscent to that of Havana; both have similar warm weather, high humidity, and an abundant of sunshine but that's pretty much where their similarities end. Everything else felt so different to me. Everywhere I looked, things looked so clean and new to me. I marveled at the contemporary infrastructure. I've never seen so many modern cars before or so many cars in general. The roads looked maintained and even. There were also numerous stores in close proximity to each other, which was so foreign to me. I never saw that before. Everything felt so alive. Suddenly, the van made a quick stop at a KFC. Naturally, I had no idea what it was or what it meant, but I knew it had to do with food because the smell of it while we waited in the drive-thru was irresistible. Out of this bucket came out the most scrumptious fried chicken I had ever seen. The two policemen ate while on our way to the detention center, and the smell of chicken filled the van with a strong aroma, and I was hypnotized like a dog wanting its owner's meal. My mouth watered with each bite they took, and I watched them the entire ride there. It was torture. Little did I know that many years later, I would find myself working for the restaurant chain, becoming a shift supervisor during my first year in college.

Once at the detention center, we were brought into a large room with a lot of other people of all different ethnicities. The guards gave the adults uniforms, and fingerprints were taken. Detainees were given different colored uniforms depending on their nationality. They also split our group up for the first time, the women and children to one side of the center and the men to another. It was the last time I saw the majority of the group. I went with my Mom to our holding cell, but it wasn't the typical immigration cell you would think looked today. We were in a section for just mothers and their children, and it wasn't overcrowded as one would think. Some of the women staying in our section would converse with Mom about their own struggles and sacrifices that led them there. So many harrowing stories were shared. Shortly after, we were told it was lunch time and we were escorted to a dining hall. I couldn't believe what they were serving......... fried chicken! To this day, I swear my energy from desiring the KFC in the van made that happen for lunch because what are the odds of that? I savored every bite of that fried chicken. While we were having our lunch, Mom recognized a man from our neighborhood from back home. This man had the contact information of my dad's side of the family that lived in Miami. Mom was able to make a phone call later that evening and communicated to one of my uncles that we were detained at Krome. By then, they'd already gotten news from Cuba that we had left Cuba on a raft. They were relieved to find out we were alive and well. They immediately told my Mom they would come to get us the next day.

LEARNING TO WALK...AGAIN

Back in Cuba, once they found out we had left the country, my family experienced a period of great uncertainty and anxiety as they waited to hear if we had successfully made it to the United States. Communication between Cuba and the United States was limited at that time, where it could take weeks or even months for news to reach families about their loved ones' fate. Families would anxiously wait for any information, sometimes relying on sporadic phone calls, letters, or rely on Radio Martí to listen to names being called out of those who made it to the U.S. The primary objective of Radio Martí was to provide news and information to the people of Cuba, offering an alternative to the state-controlled media on the island. Its programming covered a wide range of topics, including news, politics, culture, human rights, and democracy. Needless to say, the Cuban government has condemned the station, viewing it as a tool of U.S. propaganda aimed at destabilizing the regime. Listening to the programming was considered clandestine, and the government made serious efforts to jam its signals. Many families, like mine, still did what they could to get signal and listen in secrecy at night. My Mom's oldest sister, in particularly, would listen to the radio for days, along with my other aunts, trying to hear if our names were mentioned during the

LEARNING TO WALK...AGAIN

section of the programing that cited Cubans arrivals. For my family, it was a time marked by a mix of anticipation, longing, and the fear of the unknown. On one of the listens, they heard our names being called and they broke down into tears as a mixture of relief, joy and even sadness hit them all at once.

Our night at Krome wasn't the easiest for my Mom, and to this day, I feel awful about how I behaved, but I was only eight years old. Not only was my body, especially my legs, aching like crazy, but out of nowhere I had such an urge to drink milk. Back in our home country, I used to love drinking milk and would usually have a warm cup of milk before bed. I supposed when I tasted milk again on the ship after not having it for a week, it awakened that craving again and all I wanted was milk. I cried and cried for a glass of milk, and there was nothing she could do but try to console me. One of the security guards felt so bad and gave me a can of Coca-Cola, but I didn't want it. I cried myself to sleep that night.

In addition to privileges that had been established as a result of the unique political and historical circumstances surrounding Cuba and its relationship with the United States, we were also lucky to have family members in

Miami that were willing to provide us with a place to live, which was incredibly generous and beneficial for our resettlement process and also meant we could leave the detention center as soon as my family signed off on our release. It is true that Cuban immigrants have historically been granted certain privileges that are not extended to immigrants from other nationalities. Something which has created a lot of hostility towards us. And I completely get their frustration. As a Cuban, I have mixed feelings about the immigration privileges. While I acknowledge the advantages we receive, which I am so grateful for, I also recognize the disparities in treatment compared to other nationalities. I believe that all individuals, regardless of their country of origin, should be treated equally in terms of immigration policies. Having grown up in Miami since the age of eight, I've met people from all walks of life who I've gotten to know and their struggles with immigration. I have always shown solidarity and will continue to do so, because I recognize the shared experiences of migration and I would be a hypocrite if I don't support for equal treatment and opportunities for all immigrants, regardless of their nationality. On a side note, the "Wet Foot, Dry Foot" policy was modified in 2017, effectively ending the automatic granting of parole to Cuban nationals who reached U.S. soil.

LEARNING TO WALK...AGAIN

I had never met a good portion of my dad's large side of the family, as many of them came to the U.S. before I was born and others when I was just a toddler. I knew that my parents met through my dad's sisters and the family as a whole, as they all lived in the same neighborhood as my Mom's family. One of my dad's sisters in particular was one of my Mom's best friends while growing up. It was mainly through her that my Mom met my dad. They were closest in age and went to the same school. She came to the United States two years before I was born. She would send my mom baby clothes for me to help my Mom with what she could and always remained a faithful friend of hers. I had heard of her many times and felt a tremendous amount of love for her even before meeting her.

We spent a single night at the detention center, which was miraculous. My dad's side of the family kept their word and came to pick us up the next day, and we couldn't be happier. My Mom was so overwhelmed with emotions, relieved and full of gratitude. It felt like we finally had some direction for ourselves in the new country we were to call home. Again, there were some papers to be filed, then we were put in a van, and we left the center around evening time. That was the last time I ever saw the majority of the members of our raft group. Mom and I saw Jesus, our captain, on the way home from school one random day, when I was in middle school, around 1996. By chance, we stopped at a red light and when we looked over, he was in the car next to us. We pulled over and talked to him briefly, it was nice seeing him again and catch up. The only other person I have seen since was Maricel, which I got to see again as an adult at a family gathering. It was kind of surreal seeing her and talking to her about our journey all those years later. We experience something incredibly challenging together that binds us forever. To this day, I don't know much, if anything, about the rest of the group. Our lives went separate ways.

The van took us to an immigration building in the heart of Miami somewhere, and when we got there, we were greeted by two of my uncles in the parking garage. They were so excited to see us. One of them gave me this bag filled with bubblegum. I had never had bubblegum before and was so curious as to what it tasted like or how it was different than the standard chicklet gum that I had back home. As we made our way into the building, I put six pieces of bubblegum in my mouth and got into an elevator with my Mom and family. I was so preoccupied chewing that big mass of bubblegum that I wasn't prepared for what greeted us when the elevator doors opened. I don't think any of us did. A whole bunch of camera flashes momentarily blinded me as anchors and journalists from different news stations were in front of the elevator doors. They gathered around us when we stepped out and a woman by the name of Leticia Callava from Telemundo 51 News came up to me, put her microphone up to my face, and asked how old I was. I awkwardly answered her with my mouth still chewing the ball of gum. Then she asked me what I wanted to be when I grew up. I'm still not sure why I gave her the answer I did or where it came from, but I told her, "An architect." I have tried to find this footage, but I have not had any luck. It would be incredible to see myself at that age at that moment.

I got to see and meet more of my family members that were waiting for us on the immigration office floor. After more papers were filed, we finally got into my family's car and drove down one of the famous roads in Miami, Calle Ocho. A road that's filled with Cuban culture on every street corner and building, where our cultural roots are given new grounds to move free, a place that to me, symbolizes new beginnings. It was exciting. I looked at my mom with a huge smile on my face, and she looked at me; no words were needed. Some people's idea of "making it" in life is being rich, successful, famous, having lots of houses, and traveling, but for my Mom and me, it was freedom. From that moment on, it didn't matter what else happened from there on out. We made it.

CHAPTER 11

THE IMMIGRANT EXPERIENCE

"Recognize yourself in him and her who are not like you and me."

- Carlos Fuentes

THE IMMIGRANT EXPERIENCE

"Go back to your country" and "You don't belong here" sticks with a person for life and can cause so much internal shame. Yet, it's the ugly truth of the life of an immigrant in America. These words cause further division as if there weren't enough already. The ripple effect of these words can last for years until a person finds the courage to release the shame, tap into their resiliency, and connect, building their sense of belonging. For the most part, I now sound like any other American. Still, I have not forgotten what it felt like, especially for my mother, to feel "othered" and unwelcome in our new country. I endured it many times while being in school, talking in Spanish with my Mother in public, at shopping centers or riding the bus. Growing up, I had become used to being called a "Mexican." Not that there's anything wrong with being Mexican, but it was the intention behind it. It's the tone. It was said with a negative undertone in an effort to make me feel bad in some sort of way or ridicule me, dehumanize me, and dismiss me as a foreigner. Labeling all Latin American immigrants as "Mexicans" perpetuates stereotypes and fails to acknowledge the individuality and unique backgrounds of immigrants.

THE IMMIGRANT EXPERIENCE

Discrimination in the political landscape is far more severe, though equally disappointing. Newcomers to the United States have always had to navigate a path mired in divisive politics, hindered by legal obstacles, and polluted by anti-immigrant rhetoric, something that we all still deal with currently, sadly. For decades, politicians have used their platform to use inflammatory language that stereotypes and scapegoats immigrants, portraying us as a burden on society, criminals, or even threats to national security. This kind of speech can fuel negative sentiments and discrimination against our communities. It is so important to recognize that we as immigrants contribute positively to society in various ways, including through economic contributions, cultural diversity, and even enriching the social fabric of our adopted country.

Once the initial excitement of being in a new land wears off, you begin to realize how vulnerable you really are and become aware of the immense power the unfamiliar has over you. Our daily lives felt like we were in a constant disorienting state. The biggest deterrent for me and my Mother was the language barrier. The inability to communicate effectively kept us stuck and was extremely intimidating. The only word we knew how to say in English at the time was "No", by default. In the summer of 1991,

THE IMMIGRANT EXPERIENCE

I was enrolled in summer school to get a head start on learning English, and I remember my first day like it was yesterday. When I arrived in the morning, I was told to go to the back of the school, where kids of various ages gathered at a large playground to wait for the school bell to sound off and for classes to begin. The sight was frightening, to say the least. I quietly sat on the ground, trying to stay invisible. They must have immediately smelled new blood because not even five minutes after I sat there, a much older girl surrounded by other kids walked up to me and began pointing at me and laughing. To this day, I have no idea why they did this, but it only grew the feeling that something was wrong with me. It made me feel even more of an outcast than I already did. Between the language barrier and these kinds of intimidating incidents, it became hard for me connect with others and it hindered my social skills development. Also, I don't know if this played a role in the acquisition of picking up the English language but the back and forth between both English and Spanish became a challenge for me to maintain proficiency in both languages for a long time. In a way, it was hard to prioritize one language and not neglect the other one. To this day, I sometimes find myself having issues speaking clearly and with confidence. But even still, I was determined to succeed. I had to- for my Mom.

THE IMMIGRANT EXPERIENCE

I worked hard and at that age, naturally I was a sponge. That, coupled with my eagerness to learn, worked in my favor, and eventually began speaking and writing English with ease. However, for my mom, it was a different story. She simply didn't have it in her to grasp it, so the responsibility of communicating was placed on me. Navigating the language barrier with the little English I knew in the beginning was difficult, even the little nuances of trying to speak with someone over the phone. Looking back now, there are so many comical moments that resulted from these exchanges, even though, at the time, they didn't seem so funny. Whether it was at the grocery store, doctor's office, or school meetings, I helped bridge the language gap by translating conversations and even helped fill out forms for my Mother. Things got more real when we had to navigate the bureaucracy of government institutions and understand the intricacies of things like health care, insurance policies, and all the never-ending things adults must take care of. It's also scary because there's a risk of being taken advantage of by those who wish to profit from our vulnerability.

When we first arrived in the U.S., we were fortunate enough to had lived with relatives from my dad's side of the family, and they lived in what to me felt like a luxurious mansion compared to how I lived in Cuba, which made the whole experience of first getting to the U.S. seem even more like a fairytale. But not every fairytale has a happy ending. It was there that I learned that not everything is what it appears to be, and even more importantly, that time tells all. Time reveals people's differences in lifestyles and behaviors, and it's sometimes challenging to mesh those differences to a smooth order for all. My mom decided that our stay there had to end for our own growth and mental peace. Even though it wasn't an easy decision to make and, quite frankly, highly terrifying to a single mother in a foreign country, my mom still prioritized finding independence. Regardless of the outcome, Mom and I are forever grateful for everything they did for us, and I have personally decided to just treasure the good moments I experienced during my time there as opposed to focusing on the harsh and disappointing truth.

My mom got in contact with a good friend from Cuba named Carmen, and she lived in South Florida with her husband, Eduardo. They graciously opened their home doors to us, and although it was a tiny one-bedroom apartment, it was our home for the next few months. We slept on the sofa bed together, and the size or place didn't matter. We were happy to be together and, in a home, where we felt wanted and safe. By God's goodwill, an apartment in the same complex across from Carmen became available. Carmen talked the apartment manager into renting it to my mom. Carmen guided my mother and even got her a job at the same factory she worked sewing, which was great because we didn't have a car then. She would go to work with her while I attended a new school. Carmen and Eduardo treated us like family. Their generosity and support could never be repaid because no price would be enough for what they helped us accomplish. They truly aided us to get on our feet and jumpstart the new beginning we dreamed of. I love them dearly.

One of the biggest shocks for my Mother when she began to work in the U.S. was the fact that no one talked about politics in the workplace. It was such a welcome change for her. In Cuba, it was the complete opposite and something my Mother despised. When an individual begins to work in Cuba, the government makes it a priority to influence you, always. It begins early on when they try to recruit teenagers and young adults into the organization, "Unión de Jóvenes Comunistas"or Union of Young Communists. Its main objective is to train the new generations with political ideologies the state has developed throughout

THE IMMIGRANT EXPERIENCE

history, basically brainwashing the youth. Eventually this would lead to officially signing with the Communist Party and becoming a member. My Mother never accepted it. Whenever upper management or any personnel from work would ask her why she hadn't sign up to be part of the Party, she would always come up with an excuse but always did it in a way to never sound like she was an anti-revolutionary, because that could easily get you to prison. There was always constant pressure from the government for citizens to be part of the movement. Mom would witness politics manipulation first-hand. While at work in Havana, the government would suddenly shut-down the workforce and make workers get on buses that would take them to the "Plaza de la Revolución" or Revolution Square, to watch Fidel Castro make state-wide speeches. They would then cut off the transportation system to make it hard for people to leave and force them to listen to the whole thing. The government would then be able to capture large crowds "supporting" Castro while he unleashed his propaganda on live tv. My Mother would get through the crowds and literally walk home for miles, because she refused to stay and support him in any way. My Mother might have grown up with that system around her, but she never tolerated it.

THE IMMIGRANT EXPERIENCE

After a few months living with Carmen and Eduardo, we finally began renting our own place for the first time in America; a small studio-like apartment that was just $250 a month at the time but felt like thousands of dollars for us. Her newly found independence gave my Mother empowerment but it also came with a price; the parenting pressure, worries and the responsibility of balancing it all on her own. It was challenging because we were still learning to navigate the language barrier and culture shock. It was a difficult time for us, more so for my mom. Throughout the 1990's, Mom worked in warehouses that were typically minimum waged, doing jobs that did not require extensive skills or education. It was mostly repetitive and physically demanding tasks like sewing hundreds of the same pieces repeatedly and organizing inventory. In the beginning, she also had to work multiple jobs for us to not just survive but thrive. I would come home from school, and we only had a short time to spend together because she had to leave for her second job, cleaning offices in the evening. Even so, she always had dinner ready for me to warm up for later and taught me how to cook certain foods. I was able to cook an entire meal by the age of nine. I was left alone at home for most of the night, but I knew it wasn't because she wanted to be away. I knew it was a sacrifice, and I was aware of the daily strain on her shoulders. It bothered me that I wasn't old enough to help more. I would compensate by doing little things to help with what I could.

Even though I had very little, I felt like I had everything I needed. I didn't have the latest clothes or shoes, but I never asked my Mom for anything that was out of our means. Not even video game systems, even though I wanted one badly. Eventually, she surprised me and bought me my own Super Nintendo in the mid-'90s through the catalog retailer Fingerhut, for which she paid monthly installments. And I was beyond content to be playing the one game it came with, Super Mario Brothers, for many years until I was able to buy other ones on my own. When it came to my schoolwork, I prioritized being the best student I could be, not only for myself but for her. There was difficulty understanding some of the assignments because of the language hindrance, so I took it upon myself to go back to the teacher once the class was done to ask if they could go over the assignment with me one more time so that I could fully understand it before I went home. I knew my Mom didn't have the time or the knowledge to help me with it, so I understood it was my job to relieve her from that burden. It was one less thing for her to worry about. I could have gone home and told her I didn't have homework, but I was never that kid for some reason. I was determined to succeed. Something in me wanted to do it for her, to show her that her sacrifices weren't made in vain.

Between my subtle interactions at school, viewing cartoons at home, and watching shows like Full House, Family Matters, and Saved by The Bell, my English improved. Those shows were not only educational but an integral part of my childhood. These early years of my life were very lonely, and these shows helped me feel like I was part of their family. I didn't have many friends during this time- at school or at home. The apartment complex we lived in only had adult tenants without children, so I was the only kid in the entire complex. The manager made an exception for my Mom and me because of our situation. They knew I was a quiet kid, and I never wanted to jeopardize the security of our home, so I made sure to stay that way. It was such a contrast to my life in Cuba, where my neighborhood was filled with other kids, and I constantly played outside. This had a significant effect on me, and I became super closed-off.

I didn't understand it at the time, but I faced psychological trauma during those early years here. Being lost at sea, on the brink of death, is a deeply distressing experience.

It served as a stark reminder of the fragility of human life and the indomitable power of nature. The effects of all of that trauma slowly manifested itself the more I began to be away from my Mother; when she would go to work and I would go to school, for example. I would feel extremely distressed, fearing that something terrible might happen to her if we were apart. I developed significant separation anxiety, especially when I first enrolled in school and was away from her for a long period of time. I would be in class and, out of nowhere, quietly start crying. I was constantly having thoughts of death, especially of my Mom dying. I would have these sudden panic attacks where I would get agitated and experienced high anxiety levels in class, where I needed to see if my Mom was okay, making it hard for me to concentrate. I was constantly worried about her safety. A teacher noticed my behavior and asked my Mom to come to see her. They spoke about our insane ordeal of how we came to America, and she suggested we both go to therapy, but we never did. Life was too complicated, and my Mom simply couldn't find the time or the money to attend treatment. I dealt with it on my own, in my own way, and each day the fear of losing her improved, but it did last well throughout junior high school.

THE IMMIGRANT EXPERIENCE

As I mentioned earlier, I was bullied a lot. For one, I was an immigrant, didn't talk with confidence, I was smaller than my classmates, very skinny, introverted, and didn't wear "cool" clothes. And of course, there was also my sexuality. Even though I did my best to hide who I truly was, it was clear that on the surface, I still gave off a vibe that I was "different." Not only did I get mistreated by my peers, but also by adults. It might have been hurtful to deal with it on a regular basis, but I tried to never let it get to me. After all I had been through, I developed tough skin and I faced it head on. But of course, that didn't make it any easier. I never understood the reason for the bullying or what they hoped to gain out of it, but I knew that it was wrong. Bullying is never acceptable, and everyone deserves to be treated with respect and dignity, regardless of their background. Our differences and similarities as people is what makes the world a rich and diverse place. Each person has their own unique experiences, perspectives, and backgrounds that contribute to the tapestry of humanity. Embracing and celebrating these differences I think leads to greater empathy, and appreciation for one another. Our similarities also play a crucial role in fostering connections and building relationships. Despite our different backgrounds, cultures, or languages, there are fundamental aspects of being human that we all share.

THE IMMIGRANT EXPERIENCE

We all experience joy, pain, love, and sadness. We have a capacity for compassion, kindness, and understanding. Realizing these shared experiences will only help us find common ground and forge connections with one another. But we need to acknowledge and value both our differences and similarities so that we can create a more inclusive and harmonious society. I wish more people would see both the beauty of our unique perspectives and our shared humanity. It is through embracing diversity that we can learn from one another, challenge our preconceptions, and grow as individuals and communities. I think that is what makes the world a more vibrant and fascinating place to live. Recognizing and accepting this is the key to ending up with a shared understanding and appreciation of what it means to be an American.

After a couple of years of being in the United States, my Mother happened to meet another Jesus, but this time, it was someone who brough her joy and companionship into her life. After so much heartbreak and hardships, my Mom had found love again for the first time in a long time. Love has the power to heal wounds and restore faith in the possibility of a fulfilling partnership. Jesus provided that for her and we became a family. His presence and love had a positive impact on my Mother's life and on mine. I now

THE IMMIGRANT EXPERIENCE

had a stepdad who I looked up to and who filled the role of father figure I always yearned for.

I'm not going to lie, at first, it wasn't easy for me to welcome him into our lives. For so long it was just my mom and me, so I had a tough time accepting someone else in the picture. I had my reservations about him, and I didn't know how to build trust with him. What were his intentions? The moment I took notice that he was a good person didn't really take long. Hurricane Andrew was about to hit South Florida, and Jesus was staying with us. The wind was picking up when I was roaming outside our complex. I noticed there was a pigeon under a truck, and I could tell it was injured. I knew the hurricane would hit overnight and the pigeon wouldn't have shelter. I ran to my Mom and Jesus and urgently told them about the pigeon. Without hesitation, Jesus asked me to show him where the pigeon was. He was able to grab the pigeon and took it inside our apartment, made a little bed with a box and towel and the pigeon made it through the storm with us safe and sound. The following morning, we let it go free. The small action spoke volumes for me. I saw that he had a good heart and it allowed me to recognize his genuine nature and character.

THE IMMIGRANT EXPERIENCE

He came into our lives at a crucial age in my life and I'm glad he was there to guide me. My stepdad provided valuable support and direction as I navigated adolescence. I witnessed my Mother live a life of happiness like I never had before, she had truly found her soulmate. However, she also experienced great loss. You see, my Mother became pregnant with twins. Jesus longed to have children of his own. So, he and my Mom were ecstatic. We were all so happy. We began buying all sorts of baby furniture and accessories later to find out, at eight weeks into her pregnancy, my Mother suffered a miscarriage. She was taken to the hospital after experiencing pelvic pain and bleeding. At the hospital, they informed her she had lost a baby. We were all devastated. She was sent home that day, but later that night my Mother woke up screaming and crying in pain. They rushed her to the hospital where it was discovered that the hospital accidentally removed the healthy baby and left the one that was deceased. The unbelievable negligence on the hospital's part ripped our family apart. My Mother suffered great depression, some of the darkest times in our home. Because we were so new here and unfamiliar with the laws and our legal rights, we never took formal legal action. To make matters worse, my Mother was never able to get pregnant again. This caused a rift between Mom and my stepdad and as years went on, their love grew apart, eventually separating in the late 90's. My Mother never experienced love like that again. She did, however, encounter a couple of romances that never came close to replicating the emotional connection and the sense of fulfillment she felt with my ex-stepdad, but instead, helped her transition into new chapters in her life and gain personal growth.

As I grew older, I realized that the journey here to the United States gave me freedom but coming out to my Mother 16 years later truly set me free. For so long, I dealt with so much internal agony, nurturing feelings in the dark that grew over time holding me captive. I lived a life focused on pleasing others, especially when it came at the expense of my own happiness and authenticity. The societal pressures to conform to certain expectations ate away at my self-confidence. Even though it's in my nature to have concerns about other people's reactions, I also think it's important for me to remember that living authentically is crucial for my own self-acceptance and mental health. As soon as I forced myself to be truly myself and I let go of everything that had provided me comfort for so long, I changed forever. Taking that leap was transformational, it was then that I was able to be the man I was meant to be, fully present and alive. Opening about one's sexual orientation is a deeply personal decision that only one can make at their own time, but I encourage anyone going through that struggle to open up as soon as possible, at least I wish I did. Looking back, I feel that by growing up in fear and so closed off I was only doing a disservice to myself. I robbed others from getting to know the person that I truly am. I have always believed that everyone's story matters and it is important to share it with the world. That is why I am sharing mine today. I have faced many struggles and challenges throughout my life, but I have been able to find the courage and determination to overcome them. I have seen how the courage to overcome, even in small ways, can have a huge impact on the lives of others. That is why I hope that by telling my story, I can help to raise awareness of the issues faced by so many people. I hope I can provide support to those who need it and foster a sense of belonging for anyone who can benefit from hearing my perspective. Even if it's in the smallest of ways, I hope that my story will make a difference and hopefully help show others that they are not alone.

I now get to honor my mom's legacy by accomplishing all my dreams and having her by my side for the ride. She saw me graduate in the top ten percent of my high school class. I'll never forget the look on my Mom's face on the day of my graduation. It was the look of pride and pure love. My accomplishment was her accomplishment too. Me graduating with honors was significant validation to her that we not only made it but that all the sacrifices and risks she took were worth it. She also saw me graduate from college as I received my Master's degree; the first person in my family to earn a Master's. It was a very proud moment for her. My mother didn't want me to have the hardships she had when she was growing up. Even though her dreams of being who she wanted to be were cut off from a very young age, she knew the risk she took with me out at sea would eventually open the door of possibilities for me to live and realize my own. What a beautiful sentiment for a human to love someone so much that they were willing to risk so much solely for that person to have a better life.

Working since she was technically a kid, my Mother finally retired at age 67, and I now have the honor of taking care of her. There is this immense beauty and humbleness in the fact that I now get to take care of her the way she took care of me when I was a child. Call it karma or just the cycle of life, but the idea that I finally give back to my Mom a fraction of what she has given me grounds me in everything I do. Out of every being in the universe, every person in the world, I was lucky and blessed to be my Mother's son. She's my reason for being. She's my rock, my hero. I don't know a more courageous person. Growing up, I've always watched my Mom be the epitome of strength and resilience. All that I am and still hope to be, I owe to her. There just aren't enough thank you's for what she has done for me and what she represents in my life. I wrote this book mostly to shine a light on her, a single mother, who has endured hardships time and time again yet still dared to dream bigger than any of her fears. She found the strength to carve her own path by never losing sight that life can change for the better even in the face of adversity. She took ownership of her own life and maintained a strong belief in the potential for positive change and took proactive steps to create the life she desired. I hope my Mother's strength can serve as an inspiration not only for anyone facing similar challenges but especially other single mothers who often navigate their journey without the recognition or support they deserve. I hope it empowers them to continue to push through circumstances and find alternative paths to success and happiness. My Mother's unconditional love for me was the powerful force that shaped me into who I am today. She is what I strive to live up to every day and I am so fortunate to be able to call her my Mother.

THE IMMIGRANT EXPERIENCE

Sadly, in the 32 years of living in the United States, I was only able to see my dad once. He was able to visit the states and I feel like I never had a real opportunity to communicate my feelings to him and open up in the short time he was here. There was so much time that got in between our relationship, so much unsaid, so many misunderstandings, and roadblocks, that I know we needed more time together to mend our relationship. When I was a teenager, I tried to call him and his wife at the time had picked up the phone and right when I said that it was me, she hung up. I felt so confused, but I called back, and she hung up the phone on me again. I decided to call my dad one more time and this time he answered the phone. I could hear my dad upset and telling her something about it. It was an awkward conversation though, and I never understood why she had animosity towards me, and I allowed that to stop me from calling more often in the future. I regret that now more than ever as I lost my dad to Covid in 2021. There was so much I wanted to talk to him about but never did, but I find comfort in the fact that on our last video call a few weeks before his passing, our conversation felt the most natural. In a strange twist of fate, on the same year my dad passed, two of my three siblings from my dad's marriages came to America. My older brother, who I always looked up to growing up and my youngest sister who I never got to meet before, as she was born after I left Cuba. I have now been given the chance to catch up on lost time and to bond with them as siblings. It's a blessing.

I often wonder, what is my purpose in life? As I get older, I've come to understand that I don't have a singular purpose. Since I was a little boy, I let my childhood imagination be my guiding light, allowing me to get inspired and in return pursue dreams that often seemed so impossible to attain. It served as a driving force for me to seek out opportunities, gather knowledge and ultimately take the steps towards turning my dreams into reality once I got older. From the moment I arrived in America, as an immigrant kid, I felt the weight of my Mother's sacrifice on me. Not because she placed that pressure on me, but because I, myself, clearly understood the significant value of her sacrifices. But my internal battle with my sexuality prevented me from fully existing and seizing opportunities. Once I began to live authentically, it allowed me to show up and be present. It was then that I was able to carry us, my Mother and I, to new heights and reap the fruits of my Mother's sacrifices. That's the beauty of being free in this beautiful country and having the liberty to dream big and work hard for what I want. I've made it my purpose of continuing to evolve and strive for a better me with the opportunities presented to me. Whatever I choose to do, I'll try my best to do it well because it fulfills me deeply to know that my Mom's brave leap of faith single-handedly changed the course of my life for the better. Without even knowing it, she helped cleanse our bloodline from the burdens she inherited. It was her determination, resilience, and strong will that broke free from negative patterns and circumstances. It is so essential for me to acknowledge and appreciate my Mother's efforts and the positive impact it has had on me from the time I was born. By pushing past her hardships and working towards change and healing, she has set an inspiring example of resilience and personal growth.

This book is my tribute to her.

WE STAY
TOGETHER

*Hand in hand,
you said we stay together, you told them,
you told me, even when we floated
out at sea.
We stay together.*

*Hoping to find a better life, it was your voice telling me
you're there and it's going to be alright.
You were my guiding light as we were blinded by the dark
night.
The waves rolled over us, each time
taking a little bit
of our hope with them, yet,
we still fought. We stay together.*

*I've been by your side, and have seen you fight for our
lives, fight for our rights. I've seen you work day and
night,
sacrificing, giving, and struggling to make my life better.
We stay together.*

I've seen you try

*to make all the wrongs right. I've heard you cry at night. I've seen you grieve
all that you've lost along the way, and each time, I've seen you get up to face another day
so that we stay together.
Although, time has passed,
and years have graced your age, still to me, Mom, you'll always look the same.
I see your strength,
you're the strongest woman I know.*

*You're courage and wisdom have kept me anchored in this journey of life.
We stay together.*

*You pulled me out of the darkness when no one else could.
My whole life, you've continued to be
my guiding light. We stay together.*

*How can I possibly describe my gratitude
or the depths of my love for you?
I struggle to get anything out because words don't seem to be enough.
So,
I dedicate my life to your legacy, but this time,
with you by my side, because
we stay together.*

ABOUT THE AUTHOR

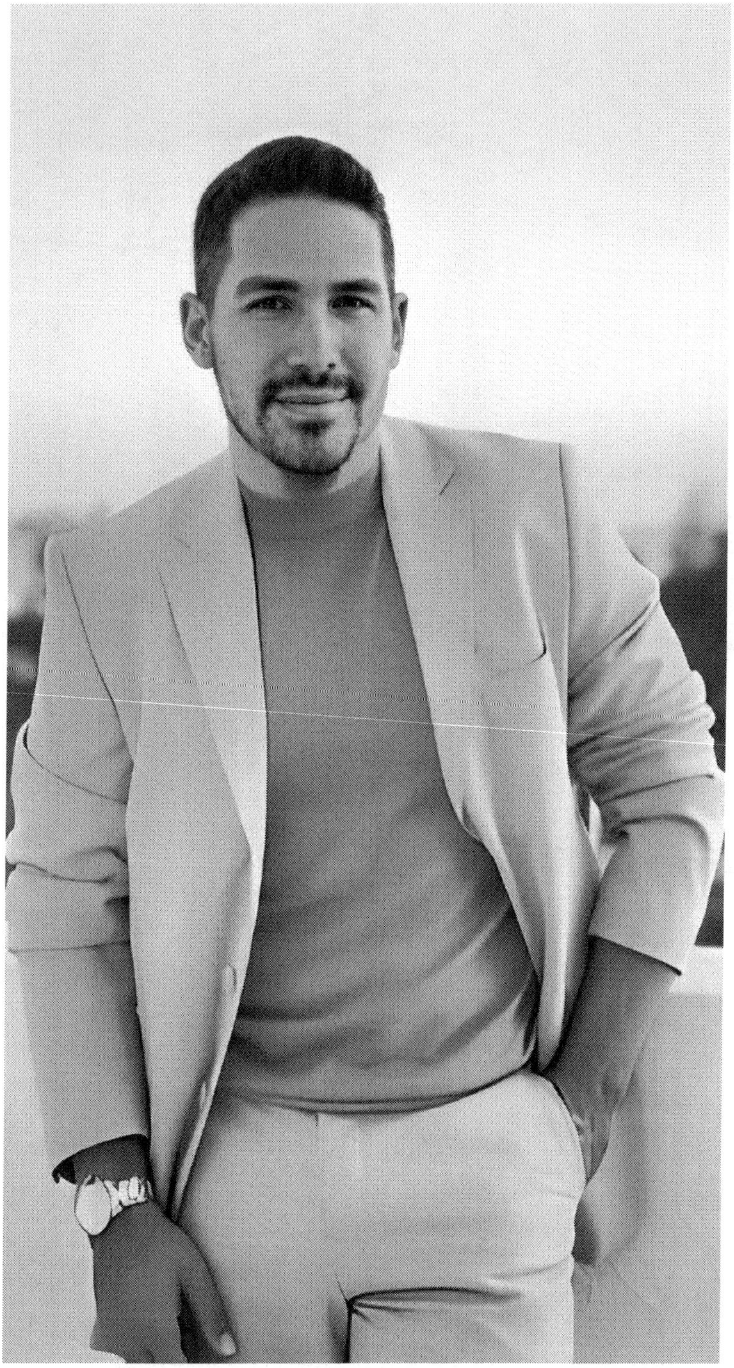

Having lived in silence most of his life, Jalyll Suarez, is on a mission to not only speak his truth but break others free from the infection of silence. Often, we feel alone in our traumas and personal struggles, but that can't be further away from the truth. Jalyll had checked so many things off the list on paper including graduating with his Master's degree, finding love and getting married, retiring his mother from work, and establishing a career for himself, yet, there was always something missing- inner peace. Jalyll hopes that sharing his story helps others to step into light to share theirs so they too can liberate themselves from self-imposed prisons that shame and fear trap us in. You can learn more about Jalyll Suarez through his website at: JalyllSuarez.com. You can also book Jalyll Suarez for speaking engagements through his email at,

jalyll.suarez@gmail.com

REFERENCES

Chapter 2

On the Peruvian Embassy in Cuba:

- Verdon, Lexie. "Thousands in Cuba Ask Peruvian Refuge." The Washington Post, 7 Apr. 1980, www.washingtonpost.com/archive/politics/1980/04/07/thousands-in-cuba-ask-peruvian-refuge/987ab70f-3cbe-4ad3-afcd-a6fcb9152d93/.

On the Mariel Boatlift:

- Carrillo, Karen J. "The Mariel Boatlift: How Cold War Politics Drove Thousands of Cubans to Florida in 1980." History, 28 Sept. 2020, www.history.com/news/mariel-boatlift-castro-carter-cold-war.

- Walsh, Edward. "U.S. to Admit Up to 3,500 Fleeing Cubans." The Washington Post, 15 Apr. 1980, www.washingtonpost.com/archive/politics/1980/04/15/us-to-admit-up-to-3500-fleeing-cubans/a2ecf248-d3c7-4f8a-8614-08dcaae4083d/.

- Tamayo, Juan O. "Castro's Blunder Led to Crisis." The Miami Herald, 23 Apr. 2000, www.latinamericanstudies.org/mariel/blunder.htm.

Chapter 3

On Fidel Castro and his legacy:

- Muscato, Christopher. "Fidel Castro: Biography, Facts & Timeline." Study.Com, 1 Jan. 2003, study.com/academy/lesson/fidel-castro-biography-facts-timeline.html.

- Farber, Samuel. "Fidel Castro'S Rule and Legacy – Part II." Against The Current, 1 Jul. 2019, againstthecurrent.org/atc201/castros-legacy/.

- Mineo, Liz. "Cuba under Fidel'S Long Shadow." The Harvard Gazette, 5 Dec. 2016, news.harvard.edu/gazette/story/2016/12/cuba-under-fidels-long-shadow/.

Chapter 9

On "The Cuban Adjustment Act" and "Wet Foot, Dry Foot" law:

- Venancio, Marikarla N., and Isabella Oliver. "Cuban Migration Is Changing, the U.S. Must Take Note." WOLA, 25 Mar. 2022, www.wola.org/analysis/cuban-migration-is-changing-us-must-note/.

Chapter 10

On the ending of the "Wet Foot, Dry Foot" law in 2017:

- Florido, Adrian. "End Of 'Wet-Foot, Dry-Foot' Means Cubans Can Join Ranks Of 'Undocumented'." National Public Radio, 15 Jan. 2017, www.wola.org/analysis/cuban-migration-is-changing-us-must-note/.

Made in the USA
Columbia, SC
19 July 2023